C-1113   CAREER EXAMINATION SERIES

This is your
PASSBOOK for...

Assistant Social Worker

Test Preparation Study Guide
Questions & Answers

COPYRIGHT NOTICE

This book is SOLELY intended for, is sold ONLY to, and its use is RESTRICTED to individual, bona fide applicants or candidates who qualify by virtue of having seriously filed applications for appropriate license, certificate, professional and/or promotional advancement, higher school matriculation, scholarship, or other legitimate requirements of education and/or governmental authorities.

This book is NOT intended for use, class instruction, tutoring, training, duplication, copying, reprinting, excerption, or adaptation, etc., by:

1) Other publishers
2) Proprietors and/or Instructors of "Coaching" and/or Preparatory Courses
3) Personnel and/or Training Divisions of commercial, industrial, and governmental organizations
4) Schools, colleges, or universities and/or their departments and staffs, including teachers and other personnel
5) Testing Agencies or Bureaus
6) Study groups which seek by the purchase of a single volume to copy and/or duplicate and/or adapt this material for use by the group as a whole without having purchased individual volumes for each of the members of the group
7) Et al.

Such persons would be in violation of appropriate Federal and State statutes.

PROVISION OF LICENSING AGREEMENTS – Recognized educational, commercial, industrial, and governmental institutions and organizations, and others legitimately engaged in educational pursuits, including training, testing, and measurement activities, may address request for a licensing agreement to the copyright owners, who will determine whether, and under what conditions, including fees and charges, the materials in this book may be used them. In other words, a licensing facility exists for the legitimate use of the material in this book on other than an individual basis. However, It is asseverated and affirmed here that the material in this book CANNOT be used without the receipt of the express permission of such a licensing agreement from the Publishers. Inquiries re licensing should be addressed to the company, attention rights and permissions department.

All rights reserved, including the right of reproduction in whole or in part, in any form or by any means, electronic or mechanical, including photocopying, recording, or by any information storage and retrieval system, without permission in writing from the Publisher.

Copyright © 2025 by
National Learning Corporation

212 Michael Drive, Syosset, NY 11791
(516) 921-8888 • www.passbooks.com
E-mail: info@passbooks.com

PASSBOOK® SERIES

THE *PASSBOOK® SERIES* has been created to prepare applicants and candidates for the ultimate academic battlefield – the examination room.

At some time in our lives, each and every one of us may be required to take an examination – for validation, matriculation, admission, qualification, registration, certification, or licensure.

Based on the assumption that every applicant or candidate has met the basic formal educational standards, has taken the required number of courses, and read the necessary texts, the *PASSBOOK® SERIES* furnishes the one special preparation which may assure passing with confidence, instead of failing with insecurity. Examination questions – together with answers – are furnished as the basic vehicle for study so that the mysteries of the examination and its compounding difficulties may be eliminated or diminished by a sure method.

This book is meant to help you pass your examination provided that you qualify and are serious in your objective.

The entire field is reviewed through the huge store of content information which is succinctly presented through a provocative and challenging approach – the question-and-answer method.

A climate of success is established by furnishing the correct answers at the end of each test.

You soon learn to recognize types of questions, forms of questions, and patterns of questioning. You may even begin to anticipate expected outcomes.

You perceive that many questions are repeated or adapted so that you can gain acute insights, which may enable you to score many sure points.

You learn how to confront new questions, or types of questions, and to attack them confidently and work out the correct answers.

You note objectives and emphases, and recognize pitfalls and dangers, so that you may make positive educational adjustments.

Moreover, you are kept fully informed in relation to new concepts, methods, practices, and directions in the field.

You discover that you are actually taking the examination all the time: you are preparing for the examination by "taking" an examination, not by reading extraneous and/or supererogatory textbooks.

In short, this PASSBOOK®, used directedly, should be an important factor in helping you to pass your test.

ASSISTANT SOCIAL WORKER

DUTIES:
This position requires the performance of limited social work in helping patients with social, emotional and related difficulties associated with their medical condition. The work is performed under the supervision of a qualified social worker who is available either on a consulting or direct supervisory basis. Independence of action will vary depending upon whether or not the incumbent is under direct daily supervision. Employees in this class are expected to confer with professionals or agencies in or outside of the facility to obtain assistance and guidance for patients.

TYPICAL JOB DUTIES:
This position involves the performance of para-professional social work and counseling duties in helping with social, emotional and related difficulties. Work is performed under supervision of a professional social worker on a consulting or direct supervisory basis. Employees in this class are expected to meet with professionals or agencies in or outside of the facility to obtain assistance and guidance for patients.

SUBJECT OF EXAMINATION
The written test will cover knowledge, skills, and/or abilities in such areas as:
1. **Interviewing** - These questions test for knowledge of the principles and practices employed in obtaining information from individuals through structured conversations. These questions require you to apply the principles, practices, and techniques of effective interviewing to hypothetical interviewing situations. Included are questions that present a problem arising from an interviewing situation, and you must choose the most appropriate course of action to take.
2. **Preparing written material** - These questions test for the ability to present information clearly and accurately, and to organize paragraphs logically and comprehensibly. For some questions, you will be given information in two or three sentences followed by four restatements of the information. You must then choose the best version. For other questions, you will be given paragraphs with their sentences out of order. You must then choose, from four suggestions, the best order for the sentences.
3. **Principles and practices of social casework** - These questions test for knowledge of the principles and practices used in social casework. Questions may cover such topics as symptoms and treatments associated with various mental, social, and physical illnesses and disabilities; client rights and confidentiality; referral techniques; maintaining client records; establishing and maintaining relationships with clients, families, co-workers, referral agencies, and the general public; and professional and ethical concerns in casework practice.

HOW TO TAKE A TEST

I. YOU MUST PASS AN EXAMINATION

A. WHAT EVERY CANDIDATE SHOULD KNOW

Examination applicants often ask us for help in preparing for the written test. What can I study in advance? What kinds of questions will be asked? How will the test be given? How will the papers be graded?

As an applicant for a civil service examination, you may be wondering about some of these things. Our purpose here is to suggest effective methods of advance study and to describe civil service examinations.

Your chances for success on this examination can be increased if you know how to prepare. Those "pre-examination jitters" can be reduced if you know what to expect. You can even experience an adventure in good citizenship if you know why civil service exams are given.

B. WHY ARE CIVIL SERVICE EXAMINATIONS GIVEN?

Civil service examinations are important to you in two ways. As a citizen, you want public jobs filled by employees who know how to do their work. As a job seeker, you want a fair chance to compete for that job on an equal footing with other candidates. The best-known means of accomplishing this two-fold goal is the competitive examination.

Exams are widely publicized throughout the nation. They may be administered for jobs in federal, state, city, municipal, town or village governments or agencies.

Any citizen may apply, with some limitations, such as the age or residence of applicants. Your experience and education may be reviewed to see whether you meet the requirements for the particular examination. When these requirements exist, they are reasonable and applied consistently to all applicants. Thus, a competitive examination may cause you some uneasiness now, but it is your privilege and safeguard.

C. HOW ARE CIVIL SERVICE EXAMS DEVELOPED?

Examinations are carefully written by trained technicians who are specialists in the field known as "psychological measurement," in consultation with recognized authorities in the field of work that the test will cover. These experts recommend the subject matter areas or skills to be tested; only those knowledges or skills important to your success on the job are included. The most reliable books and source materials available are used as references. Together, the experts and technicians judge the difficulty level of the questions.

Test technicians know how to phrase questions so that the problem is clearly stated. Their ethics do not permit "trick" or "catch" questions. Questions may have been tried out on sample groups, or subjected to statistical analysis, to determine their usefulness.

Written tests are often used in combination with performance tests, ratings of training and experience, and oral interviews. All of these measures combine to form the best-known means of finding the right person for the right job.

II. HOW TO PASS THE WRITTEN TEST

A. NATURE OF THE EXAMINATION

To prepare intelligently for civil service examinations, you should know how they differ from school examinations you have taken. In school you were assigned certain definite pages to read or subjects to cover. The examination questions were quite detailed and usually emphasized memory. Civil service exams, on the other hand, try to discover your present ability to perform the duties of a position, plus your potentiality to learn these duties. In other words, a civil service exam attempts to predict how successful you will be. Questions cover such a broad area that they cannot be as minute and detailed as school exam questions.

In the public service similar kinds of work, or positions, are grouped together in one "class." This process is known as *position-classification*. All the positions in a class are paid according to the salary range for that class. One class title covers all of these positions, and they are all tested by the same examination.

B. FOUR BASIC STEPS

1) Study the announcement

How, then, can you know what subjects to study? Our best answer is: "Learn as much as possible about the class of positions for which you've applied." The exam will test the knowledge, skills and abilities needed to do the work.

Your most valuable source of information about the position you want is the official exam announcement. This announcement lists the training and experience qualifications. Check these standards and apply only if you come reasonably close to meeting them.

The brief description of the position in the examination announcement offers some clues to the subjects which will be tested. Think about the job itself. Review the duties in your mind. Can you perform them, or are there some in which you are rusty? Fill in the blank spots in your preparation.

Many jurisdictions preview the written test in the exam announcement by including a section called "Knowledge and Abilities Required," "Scope of the Examination," or some similar heading. Here you will find out specifically what fields will be tested.

2) Review your own background

Once you learn in general what the position is all about, and what you need to know to do the work, ask yourself which subjects you already know fairly well and which need improvement. You may wonder whether to concentrate on improving your strong areas or on building some background in your fields of weakness. When the announcement has specified "some knowledge" or "considerable knowledge," or has used adjectives like "beginning principles of..." or "advanced ... methods," you can get a clue as to the number and difficulty of questions to be asked in any given field. More questions, and hence broader coverage, would be included for those subjects which are more important in the work. Now weigh your strengths and weaknesses against the job requirements and prepare accordingly.

3) Determine the level of the position

Another way to tell how intensively you should prepare is to understand the level of the job for which you are applying. Is it the entering level? In other words, is this the position in which beginners in a field of work are hired? Or is it an intermediate or advanced level? Sometimes this is indicated by such words as "Junior" or "Senior" in the class title. Other jurisdictions use Roman numerals to designate the level – Clerk I, Clerk II, for example. The word "Supervisor" sometimes appears in the title. If the level is not indicated by the title, check the description of duties. Will you be working under very close supervision, or will you have responsibility for independent decisions in this work?

4) Choose appropriate study materials

Now that you know the subjects to be examined and the relative amount of each subject to be covered, you can choose suitable study materials. For beginning level jobs, or even advanced ones, if you have a pronounced weakness in some aspect of your training, read a modern, standard textbook in that field. Be sure it is up to date and has general coverage. Such books are normally available at your library, and the librarian will be glad to help you locate one. For entry-level positions, questions of appropriate difficulty are chosen – neither highly advanced questions, nor those too simple. Such questions require careful thought but not advanced training.

If the position for which you are applying is technical or advanced, you will read more advanced, specialized material. If you are already familiar with the basic principles of your field, elementary textbooks would waste your time. Concentrate on advanced textbooks and technical periodicals. Think through the concepts and review difficult problems in your field.

These are all general sources. You can get more ideas on your own initiative, following these leads. For example, training manuals and publications of the government agency which employs workers in your field can be useful, particularly for technical and professional positions. A letter or visit to the government department involved may result in more specific study suggestions, and certainly will provide you with a more definite idea of the exact nature of the position you are seeking.

III. KINDS OF TESTS

Tests are used for purposes other than measuring knowledge and ability to perform specified duties. For some positions, it is equally important to test ability to make adjustments to new situations or to profit from training. In others, basic mental abilities not dependent on information are essential. Questions which test these things may not appear as pertinent to the duties of the position as those which test for knowledge and information. Yet they are often highly important parts of a fair examination. For very general questions, it is almost impossible to help you direct your study efforts. What we can do is to point out some of the more common of these general abilities needed in public service positions and describe some typical questions.

1) General information

Broad, general information has been found useful for predicting job success in some kinds of work. This is tested in a variety of ways, from vocabulary lists to questions about current events. Basic background in some field of work, such as sociology or economics, may be sampled in a group of questions. Often these are principles which have become familiar to most persons through exposure rather than through formal training. It is difficult to advise you how to study for these questions; being alert to the world around you is our best suggestion.

2) Verbal ability

An example of an ability needed in many positions is verbal or language ability. Verbal ability is, in brief, the ability to use and understand words. Vocabulary and grammar tests are typical measures of this ability. Reading comprehension or paragraph interpretation questions are common in many kinds of civil service tests. You are given a paragraph of written material and asked to find its central meaning.

3) Numerical ability

Number skills can be tested by the familiar arithmetic problem, by checking paired lists of numbers to see which are alike and which are different, or by interpreting charts and graphs. In the latter test, a graph may be printed in the test booklet which you are asked to use as the basis for answering questions.

4) Observation

A popular test for law-enforcement positions is the observation test. A picture is shown to you for several minutes, then taken away. Questions about the picture test your ability to observe both details and larger elements.

5) Following directions

In many positions in the public service, the employee must be able to carry out written instructions dependably and accurately. You may be given a chart with several columns, each column listing a variety of information. The questions require you to carry out directions involving the information given in the chart.

6) Skills and aptitudes

Performance tests effectively measure some manual skills and aptitudes. When the skill is one in which you are trained, such as typing or shorthand, you can practice. These tests are often very much like those given in business school or high school courses. For many of the other skills and aptitudes, however, no short-time preparation can be made. Skills and abilities natural to you or that you have developed throughout your lifetime are being tested.

Many of the general questions just described provide all the data needed to answer the questions and ask you to use your reasoning ability to find the answers. Your best preparation for these tests, as well as for tests of facts and ideas, is to be at your physical and mental best. You, no doubt, have your own methods of getting into an exam-taking mood and keeping "in shape." The next section lists some ideas on this subject.

IV. KINDS OF QUESTIONS

Only rarely is the "essay" question, which you answer in narrative form, used in civil service tests. Civil service tests are usually of the short-answer type. Full instructions for answering these questions will be given to you at the examination. But in case this is your first experience with short-answer questions and separate answer sheets, here is what you need to know:

1) Multiple-choice Questions

Most popular of the short-answer questions is the "multiple choice" or "best answer" question. It can be used, for example, to test for factual knowledge, ability to solve problems or judgment in meeting situations found at work.

A multiple-choice question is normally one of three types—
- It can begin with an incomplete statement followed by several possible endings. You are to find the one ending which *best* completes the statement, although some of the others may not be entirely wrong.
- It can also be a complete statement in the form of a question which is answered by choosing one of the statements listed.

- It can be in the form of a problem – again you select the best answer.

Here is an example of a multiple-choice question with a discussion which should give you some clues as to the method for choosing the right answer:

When an employee has a complaint about his assignment, the action which will *best* help him overcome his difficulty is to
  A. discuss his difficulty with his coworkers
  B. take the problem to the head of the organization
  C. take the problem to the person who gave him the assignment
  D. say nothing to anyone about his complaint

In answering this question, you should study each of the choices to find which is best. Consider choice "A" – Certainly an employee may discuss his complaint with fellow employees, but no change or improvement can result, and the complaint remains unresolved. Choice "B" is a poor choice since the head of the organization probably does not know what assignment you have been given, and taking your problem to him is known as "going over the head" of the supervisor. The supervisor, or person who made the assignment, is the person who can clarify it or correct any injustice. Choice "C" is, therefore, correct. To say nothing, as in choice "D," is unwise. Supervisors have and interest in knowing the problems employees are facing, and the employee is seeking a solution to his problem.

2) True/False Questions

The "true/false" or "right/wrong" form of question is sometimes used. Here a complete statement is given. Your job is to decide whether the statement is right or wrong.

SAMPLE: A roaming cell-phone call to a nearby city costs less than a non-roaming call to a distant city.

This statement is wrong, or false, since roaming calls are more expensive.

This is not a complete list of all possible question forms, although most of the others are variations of these common types. You will always get complete directions for answering questions. Be sure you understand *how* to mark your answers – ask questions until you do.

V. RECORDING YOUR ANSWERS

Computer terminals are used more and more today for many different kinds of exams.
For an examination with very few applicants, you may be told to record your answers in the test booklet itself. Separate answer sheets are much more common. If this separate answer sheet is to be scored by machine – and this is often the case – it is highly important that you mark your answers correctly in order to get credit.
An electronic scoring machine is often used in civil service offices because of the speed with which papers can be scored. Machine-scored answer sheets must be marked with a pencil, which will be given to you. This pencil has a high graphite content which responds to the electronic scoring machine. As a matter of fact, stray dots may register as answers, so do not let your pencil rest on the answer sheet while you are pondering the correct answer. Also, if your pencil lead breaks or is otherwise defective, ask for another.

Since the answer sheet will be dropped in a slot in the scoring machine, be careful not to bend the corners or get the paper crumpled.

The answer sheet normally has five vertical columns of numbers, with 30 numbers to a column. These numbers correspond to the question numbers in your test booklet. After each number, going across the page are four or five pairs of dotted lines. These short dotted lines have small letters or numbers above them. The first two pairs may also have a "T" or "F" above the letters. This indicates that the first two pairs only are to be used if the questions are of the true-false type. If the questions are multiple choice, disregard the "T" and "F" and pay attention only to the small letters or numbers.

Answer your questions in the manner of the sample that follows:

32. The largest city in the United States is
    A. Washington, D.C.
    B. New York City
    C. Chicago
    D. Detroit
    E. San Francisco

1) Choose the answer you think is best. (New York City is the largest, so "B" is correct.)
2) Find the row of dotted lines numbered the same as the question you are answering. (Find row number 32)
3) Find the pair of dotted lines corresponding to the answer. (Find the pair of lines under the mark "B.")
4) Make a solid black mark between the dotted lines.

VI. BEFORE THE TEST

Common sense will help you find procedures to follow to get ready for an examination. Too many of us, however, overlook these sensible measures. Indeed, nervousness and fatigue have been found to be the most serious reasons why applicants fail to do their best on civil service tests. Here is a list of reminders:

- Begin your preparation early – Don't wait until the last minute to go scurrying around for books and materials or to find out what the position is all about.
- Prepare continuously – An hour a night for a week is better than an all-night cram session. This has been definitely established. What is more, a night a week for a month will return better dividends than crowding your study into a shorter period of time.
- Locate the place of the exam – You have been sent a notice telling you when and where to report for the examination. If the location is in a different town or otherwise unfamiliar to you, it would be well to inquire the best route and learn something about the building.
- Relax the night before the test – Allow your mind to rest. Do not study at all that night. Plan some mild recreation or diversion; then go to bed early and get a good night's sleep.
- Get up early enough to make a leisurely trip to the place for the test – This way unforeseen events, traffic snarls, unfamiliar buildings, etc. will not upset you.
- Dress comfortably – A written test is not a fashion show. You will be known by number and not by name, so wear something comfortable.

- Leave excess paraphernalia at home – Shopping bags and odd bundles will get in your way. You need bring only the items mentioned in the official notice you received; usually everything you need is provided. Do not bring reference books to the exam. They will only confuse those last minutes and be taken away from you when in the test room.
- Arrive somewhat ahead of time – If because of transportation schedules you must get there very early, bring a newspaper or magazine to take your mind off yourself while waiting.
- Locate the examination room – When you have found the proper room, you will be directed to the seat or part of the room where you will sit. Sometimes you are given a sheet of instructions to read while you are waiting. Do not fill out any forms until you are told to do so; just read them and be prepared.
- Relax and prepare to listen to the instructions
- If you have any physical problem that may keep you from doing your best, be sure to tell the test administrator. If you are sick or in poor health, you really cannot do your best on the exam. You can come back and take the test some other time.

VII. AT THE TEST

The day of the test is here and you have the test booklet in your hand. The temptation to get going is very strong. Caution! There is more to success than knowing the right answers. You must know how to identify your papers and understand variations in the type of short-answer question used in this particular examination. Follow these suggestions for maximum results from your efforts:

1) Cooperate with the monitor

The test administrator has a duty to create a situation in which you can be as much at ease as possible. He will give instructions, tell you when to begin, check to see that you are marking your answer sheet correctly, and so on. He is not there to guard you, although he will see that your competitors do not take unfair advantage. He wants to help you do your best.

2) Listen to all instructions

Don't jump the gun! Wait until you understand all directions. In most civil service tests you get more time than you need to answer the questions. So don't be in a hurry. Read each word of instructions until you clearly understand the meaning. Study the examples, listen to all announcements and follow directions. Ask questions if you do not understand what to do.

3) Identify your papers

Civil service exams are usually identified by number only. You will be assigned a number; you must not put your name on your test papers. Be sure to copy your number correctly. Since more than one exam may be given, copy your exact examination title.

4) Plan your time

Unless you are told that a test is a "speed" or "rate of work" test, speed itself is usually not important. Time enough to answer all the questions will be provided, but this does not mean that you have all day. An overall time limit has been set. Divide the total time (in minutes) by the number of questions to determine the approximate time you have for each question.

5) Do not linger over difficult questions

If you come across a difficult question, mark it with a paper clip (useful to have along) and come back to it when you have been through the booklet. One caution if you do this – be sure to skip a number on your answer sheet as well. Check often to be sure that you have not lost your place and that you are marking in the row numbered the same as the question you are answering.

6) Read the questions

Be sure you know what the question asks! Many capable people are unsuccessful because they failed to *read* the questions correctly.

7) Answer all questions

Unless you have been instructed that a penalty will be deducted for incorrect answers, it is better to guess than to omit a question.

8) Speed tests

It is often better NOT to guess on speed tests. It has been found that on timed tests people are tempted to spend the last few seconds before time is called in marking answers at random – without even reading them – in the hope of picking up a few extra points. To discourage this practice, the instructions may warn you that your score will be "corrected" for guessing. That is, a penalty will be applied. The incorrect answers will be deducted from the correct ones, or some other penalty formula will be used.

9) Review your answers

If you finish before time is called, go back to the questions you guessed or omitted to give them further thought. Review other answers if you have time.

10) Return your test materials

If you are ready to leave before others have finished or time is called, take ALL your materials to the monitor and leave quietly. Never take any test material with you. The monitor can discover whose papers are not complete, and taking a test booklet may be grounds for disqualification.

VIII. EXAMINATION TECHNIQUES

1) Read the general instructions carefully. These are usually printed on the first page of the exam booklet. As a rule, these instructions refer to the timing of the examination; the fact that you should not start work until the signal and must stop work at a signal, etc. If there are any *special* instructions, such as a choice of questions to be answered, make sure that you note this instruction carefully.

2) When you are ready to start work on the examination, that is as soon as the signal has been given, read the instructions to each question booklet, underline any key words or phrases, such as *least, best, outline, describe* and the like. In this way you will tend to answer as requested rather than discover on reviewing your paper that you *listed without describing*, that you selected the *worst* choice rather than the *best* choice, etc.

3) If the examination is of the objective or multiple-choice type – that is, each question will also give a series of possible answers: A, B, C or D, and you are called upon to select the best answer and write the letter next to that answer on your answer paper – it is advisable to start answering each question in turn. There may be anywhere from 50 to 100 such questions in the three or four hours allotted and you can see how much time would be taken if you read through all the questions before beginning to answer any. Furthermore, if you come across a question or group of questions which you know would be difficult to answer, it would undoubtedly affect your handling of all the other questions.

4) If the examination is of the essay type and contains but a few questions, it is a moot point as to whether you should read all the questions before starting to answer any one. Of course, if you are given a choice – say five out of seven and the like – then it is essential to read all the questions so you can eliminate the two that are most difficult. If, however, you are asked to answer all the questions, there may be danger in trying to answer the easiest one first because you may find that you will spend too much time on it. The best technique is to answer the first question, then proceed to the second, etc.

5) Time your answers. Before the exam begins, write down the time it started, then add the time allowed for the examination and write down the time it must be completed, then divide the time available somewhat as follows:
    - If 3-1/2 hours are allowed, that would be 210 minutes. If you have 80 objective-type questions, that would be an average of 2-1/2 minutes per question. Allow yourself no more than 2 minutes per question, or a total of 160 minutes, which will permit about 50 minutes to review.
    - If for the time allotment of 210 minutes there are 7 essay questions to answer, that would average about 30 minutes a question. Give yourself only 25 minutes per question so that you have about 35 minutes to review.

6) The most important instruction is to *read each question* and make sure you know what is wanted. The second most important instruction is to *time yourself properly* so that you answer every question. The third most important instruction is to *answer every question*. Guess if you have to but include something for each question. Remember that you will receive no credit for a blank and will probably receive some credit if you write something in answer to an essay question. If you guess a letter – say "B" for a multiple-choice question – you may have guessed right. If you leave a blank as an answer to a multiple-choice question, the examiners may respect your feelings but it will not add a point to your score. Some exams may penalize you for wrong answers, so in such cases *only*, you may not want to guess unless you have some basis for your answer.

7) Suggestions
    a. Objective-type questions
        1. Examine the question booklet for proper sequence of pages and questions
        2. Read all instructions carefully
        3. Skip any question which seems too difficult; return to it after all other questions have been answered
        4. Apportion your time properly; do not spend too much time on any single question or group of questions

5. Note and underline key words – *all, most, fewest, least, best, worst, same, opposite,* etc.
6. Pay particular attention to negatives
7. Note unusual option, e.g., unduly long, short, complex, different or similar in content to the body of the question
8. Observe the use of "hedging" words – *probably, may, most likely,* etc.
9. Make sure that your answer is put next to the same number as the question
10. Do not second-guess unless you have good reason to believe the second answer is definitely more correct
11. Cross out original answer if you decide another answer is more accurate; do not erase until you are ready to hand your paper in
12. Answer all questions; guess unless instructed otherwise
13. Leave time for review

   b. Essay questions
      1. Read each question carefully
      2. Determine exactly what is wanted. Underline key words or phrases.
      3. Decide on outline or paragraph answer
      4. Include many different points and elements unless asked to develop any one or two points or elements
      5. Show impartiality by giving pros and cons unless directed to select one side only
      6. Make and write down any assumptions you find necessary to answer the questions
      7. Watch your English, grammar, punctuation and choice of words
      8. Time your answers; don't crowd material

8) Answering the essay question

Most essay questions can be answered by framing the specific response around several key words or ideas. Here are a few such key words or ideas:

M's: manpower, materials, methods, money, management
P's: purpose, program, policy, plan, procedure, practice, problems, pitfalls, personnel, public relations

   a. Six basic steps in handling problems:
      1. Preliminary plan and background development
      2. Collect information, data and facts
      3. Analyze and interpret information, data and facts
      4. Analyze and develop solutions as well as make recommendations
      5. Prepare report and sell recommendations
      6. Install recommendations and follow up effectiveness

   b. Pitfalls to avoid
      1. *Taking things for granted* – A statement of the situation does not necessarily imply that each of the elements is necessarily true; for example, a complaint may be invalid and biased so that all that can be taken for granted is that a complaint has been registered

2. *Considering only one side of a situation* – Wherever possible, indicate several alternatives and then point out the reasons you selected the best one
3. *Failing to indicate follow up* – Whenever your answer indicates action on your part, make certain that you will take proper follow-up action to see how successful your recommendations, procedures or actions turn out to be
4. *Taking too long in answering any single question* – Remember to time your answers properly

IX. AFTER THE TEST

Scoring procedures differ in detail among civil service jurisdictions although the general principles are the same. Whether the papers are hand-scored or graded by machine we have described, they are nearly always graded by number. That is, the person who marks the paper knows only the number – never the name – of the applicant. Not until all the papers have been graded will they be matched with names. If other tests, such as training and experience or oral interview ratings have been given, scores will be combined. Different parts of the examination usually have different weights. For example, the written test might count 60 percent of the final grade, and a rating of training and experience 40 percent. In many jurisdictions, veterans will have a certain number of points added to their grades.

After the final grade has been determined, the names are placed in grade order and an eligible list is established. There are various methods for resolving ties between those who get the same final grade – probably the most common is to place first the name of the person whose application was received first. Job offers are made from the eligible list in the order the names appear on it. You will be notified of your grade and your rank as soon as all these computations have been made. This will be done as rapidly as possible.

People who are found to meet the requirements in the announcement are called "eligibles." Their names are put on a list of eligible candidates. An eligible's chances of getting a job depend on how high he stands on this list and how fast agencies are filling jobs from the list.

When a job is to be filled from a list of eligibles, the agency asks for the names of people on the list of eligibles for that job. When the civil service commission receives this request, it sends to the agency the names of the three people highest on this list. Or, if the job to be filled has specialized requirements, the office sends the agency the names of the top three persons who meet these requirements from the general list.

The appointing officer makes a choice from among the three people whose names were sent to him. If the selected person accepts the appointment, the names of the others are put back on the list to be considered for future openings.

That is the rule in hiring from all kinds of eligible lists, whether they are for typist, carpenter, chemist, or something else. For every vacancy, the appointing officer has his choice of any one of the top three eligibles on the list. This explains why the person whose name is on top of the list sometimes does not get an appointment when some of the persons lower on the list do. If the appointing officer chooses the second or third eligible, the No. 1 eligible does not get a job at once, but stays on the list until he is appointed or the list is terminated.

X. HOW TO PASS THE INTERVIEW TEST

The examination for which you applied requires an oral interview test. You have already taken the written test and you are now being called for the interview test – the final part of the formal examination.

You may think that it is not possible to prepare for an interview test and that there are no procedures to follow during an interview. Our purpose is to point out some things you can do in advance that will help you and some good rules to follow and pitfalls to avoid while you are being interviewed.

What is an interview supposed to test?

The written examination is designed to test the technical knowledge and competence of the candidate; the oral is designed to evaluate intangible qualities, not readily measured otherwise, and to establish a list showing the relative fitness of each candidate – as measured against his competitors – for the position sought. Scoring is not on the basis of "right" and "wrong," but on a sliding scale of values ranging from "not passable" to "outstanding." As a matter of fact, it is possible to achieve a relatively low score without a single "incorrect" answer because of evident weakness in the qualities being measured.

Occasionally, an examination may consist entirely of an oral test – either an individual or a group oral. In such cases, information is sought concerning the technical knowledges and abilities of the candidate, since there has been no written examination for this purpose. More commonly, however, an oral test is used to supplement a written examination.

Who conducts interviews?

The composition of oral boards varies among different jurisdictions. In nearly all, a representative of the personnel department serves as chairman. One of the members of the board may be a representative of the department in which the candidate would work. In some cases, "outside experts" are used, and, frequently, a businessman or some other representative of the general public is asked to serve. Labor and management or other special groups may be represented. The aim is to secure the services of experts in the appropriate field.

However the board is composed, it is a good idea (and not at all improper or unethical) to ascertain in advance of the interview who the members are and what groups they represent. When you are introduced to them, you will have some idea of their backgrounds and interests, and at least you will not stutter and stammer over their names.

What should be done before the interview?

While knowledge about the board members is useful and takes some of the surprise element out of the interview, there is other preparation which is more substantive. It *is* possible to prepare for an oral interview – in several ways:

1) Keep a copy of your application and review it carefully before the interview

This may be the only document before the oral board, and the starting point of the interview. Know what education and experience you have listed there, and the sequence and dates of all of it. Sometimes the board will ask you to review the highlights of your experience for them; you should not have to hem and haw doing it.

2) Study the class specification and the examination announcement

Usually, the oral board has one or both of these to guide them. The qualities, characteristics or knowledges required by the position sought are stated in these documents. They offer valuable clues as to the nature of the oral interview. For example, if the job involves supervisory responsibilities, the announcement will usually indicate that knowledge of modern supervisory methods and the qualifications of the candidate as a supervisor will be tested. If so, you can expect such questions, frequently in the form of a hypothetical situation which you are expected to solve. NEVER go into an oral without knowledge of the duties and responsibilities of the job you seek.

3) Think through each qualification required

Try to visualize the kind of questions you would ask if you were a board member. How well could you answer them? Try especially to appraise your own knowledge and background in each area, *measured against the job sought*, and identify any areas in which you are weak. Be critical and realistic – do not flatter yourself.

4) Do some general reading in areas in which you feel you may be weak

For example, if the job involves supervision and your past experience has NOT, some general reading in supervisory methods and practices, particularly in the field of human relations, might be useful. Do NOT study agency procedures or detailed manuals. The oral board will be testing your understanding and capacity, not your memory.

5) Get a good night's sleep and watch your general health and mental attitude

You will want a clear head at the interview. Take care of a cold or any other minor ailment, and of course, no hangovers.

What should be done on the day of the interview?

Now comes the day of the interview itself. Give yourself plenty of time to get there. Plan to arrive somewhat ahead of the scheduled time, particularly if your appointment is in the fore part of the day. If a previous candidate fails to appear, the board might be ready for you a bit early. By early afternoon an oral board is almost invariably behind schedule if there are many candidates, and you may have to wait. Take along a book or magazine to read, or your application to review, but leave any extraneous material in the waiting room when you go in for your interview. In any event, relax and compose yourself.

The matter of dress is important. The board is forming impressions about you – from your experience, your manners, your attitude, and your appearance. Give your personal appearance careful attention. Dress your best, but not your flashiest. Choose conservative, appropriate clothing, and be sure it is immaculate. This is a business interview, and your appearance should indicate that you regard it as such. Besides, being well groomed and properly dressed will help boost your confidence.

Sooner or later, someone will call your name and escort you into the interview room. *This is it.* From here on you are on your own. It is too late for any more preparation. But remember, you asked for this opportunity to prove your fitness, and you are here because your request was granted.

What happens when you go in?

The usual sequence of events will be as follows: The clerk (who is often the board stenographer) will introduce you to the chairman of the oral board, who will introduce you to the other members of the board. Acknowledge the introductions before you sit down. Do not be surprised if you find a microphone facing you or a stenotypist sitting by. Oral interviews are usually recorded in the event of an appeal or other review.

Usually the chairman of the board will open the interview by reviewing the highlights of your education and work experience from your application – primarily for the benefit of the other members of the board, as well as to get the material into the record. Do not interrupt or comment unless there is an error or significant misinterpretation; if that is the case, do not hesitate. But do not quibble about insignificant matters. Also, he will usually ask you some question about your education, experience or your present job – partly to get you to start talking and to establish the interviewing "rapport." He may start the actual questioning, or turn it over to one of the other members. Frequently, each member undertakes the questioning on a particular area, one in which he is perhaps most competent, so you can expect each member to participate in the examination. Because time is limited, you may also expect some rather abrupt switches in the direction the questioning takes, so do not be upset by it. Normally, a board member will not pursue a single line of questioning unless he discovers a particular strength or weakness.

After each member has participated, the chairman will usually ask whether any member has any further questions, then will ask you if you have anything you wish to add. Unless you are expecting this question, it may floor you. Worse, it may start you off on an extended, extemporaneous speech. The board is not usually seeking more information. The question is principally to offer you a last opportunity to present further qualifications or to indicate that you have nothing to add. So, if you feel that a significant qualification or characteristic has been overlooked, it is proper to point it out in a sentence or so. Do not compliment the board on the thoroughness of their examination – they have been sketchy, and you know it. If you wish, merely say, "No thank you, I have nothing further to add." This is a point where you can "talk yourself out" of a good impression or fail to present an important bit of information. Remember, *you close the interview yourself.*

The chairman will then say, "That is all, Mr. _____, thank you." Do not be startled; the interview is over, and quicker than you think. Thank him, gather your belongings and take your leave. Save your sigh of relief for the other side of the door.

How to put your best foot forward

Throughout this entire process, you may feel that the board individually and collectively is trying to pierce your defenses, seek out your hidden weaknesses and embarrass and confuse you. Actually, this is not true. They are obliged to make an appraisal of your qualifications for the job you are seeking, and they want to see you in your best light. Remember, they must interview all candidates and a non-cooperative candidate may become a failure in spite of their best efforts to bring out his qualifications. Here are 15 suggestions that will help you:

1) Be natural – Keep your attitude confident, not cocky

If you are not confident that you can do the job, do not expect the board to be. Do not apologize for your weaknesses, try to bring out your strong points. The board is interested in a positive, not negative, presentation. Cockiness will antagonize any board member and make him wonder if you are covering up a weakness by a false show of strength.

2) Get comfortable, but don't lounge or sprawl

Sit erectly but not stiffly. A careless posture may lead the board to conclude that you are careless in other things, or at least that you are not impressed by the importance of the occasion. Either conclusion is natural, even if incorrect. Do not fuss with your clothing, a pencil or an ashtray. Your hands may occasionally be useful to emphasize a point; do not let them become a point of distraction.

3) Do not wisecrack or make small talk

This is a serious situation, and your attitude should show that you consider it as such. Further, the time of the board is limited – they do not want to waste it, and neither should you.

4) Do not exaggerate your experience or abilities

In the first place, from information in the application or other interviews and sources, the board may know more about you than you think. Secondly, you probably will not get away with it. An experienced board is rather adept at spotting such a situation, so do not take the chance.

5) If you know a board member, do not make a point of it, yet do not hide it

Certainly you are not fooling him, and probably not the other members of the board. Do not try to take advantage of your acquaintanceship – it will probably do you little good.

6) Do not dominate the interview

Let the board do that. They will give you the clues – do not assume that you have to do all the talking. Realize that the board has a number of questions to ask you, and do not try to take up all the interview time by showing off your extensive knowledge of the answer to the first one.

7) Be attentive

You only have 20 minutes or so, and you should keep your attention at its sharpest throughout. When a member is addressing a problem or question to you, give him your undivided attention. Address your reply principally to him, but do not exclude the other board members.

8) Do not interrupt

A board member may be stating a problem for you to analyze. He will ask you a question when the time comes. Let him state the problem, and wait for the question.

9) Make sure you understand the question

Do not try to answer until you are sure what the question is. If it is not clear, restate it in your own words or ask the board member to clarify it for you. However, do not haggle about minor elements.

10) Reply promptly but not hastily

A common entry on oral board rating sheets is "candidate responded readily," or "candidate hesitated in replies." Respond as promptly and quickly as you can, but do not jump to a hasty, ill-considered answer.

11) Do not be peremptory in your answers

A brief answer is proper – but do not fire your answer back. That is a losing game from your point of view. The board member can probably ask questions much faster than you can answer them.

12) Do not try to create the answer you think the board member wants

He is interested in what kind of mind you have and how it works – not in playing games. Furthermore, he can usually spot this practice and will actually grade you down on it.

13) Do not switch sides in your reply merely to agree with a board member

Frequently, a member will take a contrary position merely to draw you out and to see if you are willing and able to defend your point of view. Do not start a debate, yet do not surrender a good position. If a position is worth taking, it is worth defending.

14) Do not be afraid to admit an error in judgment if you are shown to be wrong

The board knows that you are forced to reply without any opportunity for careful consideration. Your answer may be demonstrably wrong. If so, admit it and get on with the interview.

15) Do not dwell at length on your present job

The opening question may relate to your present assignment. Answer the question but do not go into an extended discussion. You are being examined for a *new* job, not your present one. As a matter of fact, try to phrase ALL your answers in terms of the job for which you are being examined.

Basis of Rating

Probably you will forget most of these "do's" and "don'ts" when you walk into the oral interview room. Even remembering them all will not ensure you a passing grade. Perhaps you did not have the qualifications in the first place. But remembering them will help you to put your best foot forward, without treading on the toes of the board members.

Rumor and popular opinion to the contrary notwithstanding, an oral board wants you to make the best appearance possible. They know you are under pressure – but they also want to see how you respond to it as a guide to what your reaction would be under the pressures of the job you seek. They will be influenced by the degree of poise you display, the personal traits you show and the manner in which you respond.

ABOUT THIS BOOK

This book contains tests divided into Examination Sections. Go through each test, answering every question in the margin. We have also attached a sample answer sheet at the back of the book that can be removed and used. At the end of each test look at the answer key and check your answers. On the ones you got wrong, look at the right answer choice and learn. Do not fill in the answers first. Do not memorize the questions and answers, but understand the answer and principles involved. On your test, the questions will likely be different from the samples. Questions are changed and new ones added. If you understand these past questions you should have success with any changes that arise. Tests may consist of several types of questions. We have additional books on each subject should more study be advisable or necessary for you. Finally, the more you study, the better prepared you will be. This book is intended to be the last thing you study before you walk into the examination room. Prior study of relevant texts is also recommended. NLC publishes some of these in our Fundamental Series. Knowledge and good sense are important factors in passing your exam. Good luck also helps. So now study this Passbook, absorb the material contained within and take that knowledge into the examination. Then do your best to pass that exam.

EXAMINATION SECTION

EXAMINATION SECTION
TEST 1

DIRECTIONS: Each question or incomplete statement is followed by several suggested answers or completions. Select the one that BEST answers the question or completes the statement. *PRINT THE LETTER OF THE CORRECT ANSWER IN THE SPACE AT THE RIGHT.*

1. Which of the following provides the BEST rationale for increased government involvement in solving current urban problems?
    A. The cities are not so badly off as they seem to be.
    B. Additional research and experimentation is needed to develop solutions to urban problems.
    C. Our current urban problems have obvious and simple solutions.
    D. The only thing that prevents us from solving urban problems is public opinion.

1.____

2. Ethnic identity as a factor in urban America
    A. has virtually disappeared with the rapid assimilation of second and third generation immigrants
    B. has little influence on patterns of occupational mobility
    C. has become an increasingly important determinant of residential choices
    D. continues to exercise an influence on voting behavior

2.____

3. In recent years, there has been a move to decentralize the governmental structure of some of our largest cities.
The one of the following which provides the WEAKEST argument in favor of decentralization is that decentralization will help to
    A. increase administrative responsiveness to neighborhood needs
    B. promote local democracy by developing local leaders
    C. diminish conflict between communities
    D. develop community cohesion

3.____

4. The decentralization and diffusion of metropolitan areas has resulted in
    A. a dramatic decline in the overall population density of the central city
    B. spatial segregation on the basis of race, ethnicity, and class
    C. slow-down in the rate of suburban growth in comparison to central city growth
    D. benefit to persons from lower socio-economic levels by reducing the population density of the poorest sections of the central city

4.____

5. The concentration of the poor in the core areas of the modern decentralized metropolis can BEST be explained by the
    A. failure of public transport systems to follow the new multi-centered pattern of commercial and industrial dispersion
    B. absence of low-skilled jobs in outlying industrial and commercial sub centers

5.____

C. availability of inexpensive goods and services in the central city
D. need such people feel for the security of familiar surroundings

6. Of the following, the MOST serious shortcoming of urban renewal has been that it has
   A. not attempted to modernize aging downtown areas
   B. curtailed industrial and commercial expansion in the cities
   C. failed to provide adequate housing for poor families forced to move out of their old neighborhoods
   D. not stimulated public support for public housing appropriations

6.____

7. The vast majority of blacks who had migrated from the South to northern cities had done so PRIMARILY in order to
   A. join friends and relatives
   B. take specific jobs or look for work
   C. take advantage of superior educational facilities
   D. escape southern racial prejudices

7.____

8. The one of the following that is the CHIEF justification for developing area-wide planning in health care is that such planning is likely to
   A. promote effective use of a community's total health resources
   B. minimize the need for consumer participation
   C. reduce the total cost of medical care in a community
   D. reduce the number of physicians needed in a community

8.____

9. Of the following, the CHIEF reason that the gridiron design, which consists of straight vertical streets that lie perpendicular to horizontal streets, became the dominant planning motif in urban America is that it
   A. facilitated the movement of automobile traffic to central locations
   B. was a convenient and efficient form of subdividing real estate to maximize its utilization
   C. provided fixed boundaries for neighborhoods
   D. could be easily adapted to topographical variations

9.____

10. Which of the following is generally the LARGEST cost factor in acquiring and owning a home?
    A. Building materials
    B. Skilled labor
    C. Interest on mortgage
    D. Builder's profit

10.____

11. The federally funded job training programs of the 1960's were INITIALLY conceived on the assumption that
    A. the unemployed lacked the necessary skills to qualify for existing job vacancies
    B. people who dropped out of the labor force lost their motivation to work
    C. public assistance made low wage jobs unattractive to the unemployed
    D. the unemployed would not take menial jobs

11.____

12. Which of the following statements about the urban poor is ACCURATE?
    A. The proportion of poor people in central cities is the same as in suburbs.
    B. Persons under the age of eighteen constitute the largest group of poor persons.
    C. The number of poor persons living in households headed by women has declined.
    D. The majority of poor persons are in households headed by men under the age of sixty-five.

12._____

13. Which one of the following statements concerning health care in America is CORRECT?
    A. All accepted indices indicate that our general health status is higher than that of other countries.
    B. The quality of our doctors and nurses is higher than in other countries.
    C. All people have equal access to the same quality of such care.
    D. The cost of the same quality of care is lower than in most other countries.

13._____

14. Of the following, the MOST serious shortcoming of low income public housing sponsored by the federal government is that
    A. income limitations are imposed upon the tenants
    B. housing administrators place too few restrictions on tenant activities
    C. it competes with the private housing market
    D. it has been built primarily in old and dilapidated neighborhoods

14._____

15. Which of the following is the LEAST important factor contributing to the residential segregation of blacks in metropolitan areas?
    A. Violence against the black renter and homeowner in white neighborhoods
    B. Fear by whites that the economic value of their property will decline if blacks move into white neighborhoods
    C. Personal preferences of blacks and whites
    D. Fear by whites that the quality of schools will decline if blacks move into white neighborhoods

15._____

16. Which of the following is the MOST regressive form of local taxation? _____ tax.
    A. General sales   B. Property
    C. Personal income   D. Corporate income

16._____

17. The property tax has come under attack in metropolitan regions because
    A. it fails to discriminate between different types of property within a single taxing jurisdiction
    B. insufficient revenues are raised by the tax
    C. it fails to tax improvements in property
    D. the same type of property is taxed at different rates in different communities within a region

17._____

18. Advocates of the culture of poverty hypothesis maintain that remedial action should center on the
    A. discriminatory practices against minorities
    B. lack of work opportunity
    C. attitudes and behavior of the poor
    D. inequitable distribution of educational facilities

18._____

19. The one of the following statements concerning crime in our large cities which is LEAST accurate is that
    A. the readily availability of valuable goods in our affluent society has contributed to the increase in crime
    B. young people have a higher crime rate than adults
    C. the increased ability of poor persons to move about the city has contributed to the increase in crime
    D. murder, rape, and aggravated assault constitute the majority of serious crimes as defined by the F.B.I.'s Uniform Crime Reports

19._____

20. In assessing the impact of the automobile and public mass transportation on urban population congestion, it is MOST accurate to state that
    A. the construction of an elaborate metropolitan expressway system will relieve such congestion
    B. neither the automobile nor public mass transportation can relieve such congestion
    C. adequate knowledge about the relationship between such congestion and various modes of transportation is still lacking
    D. both the automobile and public mass transportation promote such congestion

20._____

21. The Supreme Court, in March 1973, reversed previous lower court decisions which had tried to establish that the financing of education through local property taxes was unconstitutional.
    These lower court decisions were based on the contention that
    A. the property tax was applied inequitably in certain areas
    B. the property tax is not an important source of local revenues
    C. the quality of a child's education was dependent on the wealth of the community
    D. districts with a small tax base would have to add a *value added tax*

21._____

22. The percentage of local revenues which is spent on schools is smaller in urban communities than it is in suburban communities PRIMARILY because
    A. the need for quality education is not as well recognized in urban communities
    B. the tax base of urban communities is insufficient
    C. other public services in urban communities absorb a larger proportion of available funds
    D. commercial enterprises do not pay school taxes

22._____

23. The one of the following which BEST describes the trend of the drop-out rate in public high schools during the last five years is that this rate
    A. rose sharply
    B. showed little fluctuation throughout the period and ended at the same level this year as it was five years ago
    C. declined sharply
    D. showed considerable fluctuation throughout the period and ended at the same level this year as it was five years ago

24. One of the findings of the Coleman Report, EQUALITY OF EDUCATIONAL OPPORTUNITY, was that the degree to which black students felt they could affect their environment and future is related to their achievement AND to the
    A. quality of the teaching staff
    B. number of college preparatory courses offered at the high school level
    C. condition of physical facilities
    D. proportion of whites in the school

25. The concept of cultural pluralism is MOST actively opposed by
    A. the Amish
    B. supporters of black studies as a discipline
    C. supporters of bilingual education
    D. supporters of parochial schools

KEY (CORRECT ANSWERS)

1.	B		11.	A
2.	D		12.	B
3.	C		13.	B
4.	D		14.	D
5.	A		15.	A
6.	C		16.	A
7.	B		17.	D
8.	A		18.	C
9.	B		19.	D
10.	C		20.	C

21. C
22. C
23. A
24. D
25. A

TEST 2

DIRECTIONS: Each question or incomplete statement is followed by several suggested answers or completions. Select the one that BEST answers the question or completes the statement. *PRINT THE LETTER OF THE CORRECT ANSWER IN THE SPACE AT THE RIGHT.*

1. When police provide patrol services on the basis of workload, a high concentration of patrol officers in minority group neighborhoods often results. The police then are subject to criticism both from minority residents who feel persecuted by the police and from residents of other neighborhoods who feel they are not receiving the same level of police protection.
Which one of the following BEST states both whether or not, under these conditions, patrol distribution should be changed and also the BEST reason therefor?
It should
    A. *not be changed*, because community pressure should not be allowed to influence police decisions
    B. *be changed*, because all neighborhoods in the community are entitled to the same level of police protection
    C. *be changed*, because it is necessary for the police to respond to community pressures in order to improve community relations
    D. *not be changed*, because having police concentration in minority neighborhoods protects the remainder of the community from riot situations
    E. *not be changed*, because to do so would deprive law-abiding minority neighborhood residents of police protection to their need

1.____

2. A certain boy is raised by parents who are concerned with status, social position the *right* occupation, the *right* friends, the *right* neighborhood, etc. Social behavior plays a vital role in their lives, and their outlook with regard to rearing children can best be summed up by *children should be seen and not heard*. Following are four descriptive terms their son might possibly be likely to use if he were asked to describe the *perfect boy*:
   I. Being polite   II. Being a good companion
   III. Being clean   IV. Being fun
Which one of the following choices MOST accurately classifies the above statements into those the boy is MOST likely to use when describing the *perfect boy* and those which he is LEAST likely to use?
He is
    A. most likely to use I and II and least likely to use III and IV
    B. most likely to use I and III and least likely to use II and IV
    C. most likely to use I, II, and III and least likely to use IV
    D. most likely to use II and IV and least likely to use I and III
    E. equally likely to use any of I, II, III, and IV

2.____

6

3. People adjust to frustrations or conflicts in many different words. One of these ways of adjustment is known as projection.
Which one of the following behaviors is the BEST example of projection?
A person
   A. who is properly arrested for inciting a riot protests against police brutality and violence
   B. stopped for going through a red light claims that he couldn't help it because his brakes wouldn't hold
   C. who is arrested for a crime persistently claims to have forgotten the whole incident that led to his arrest
   D. who is arrested for a crime cries, screams, and stamps his feet on the floor like a child having a temper tantrum
   E. who is stopped for a traffic violation claims that he is a close friend of the mayor in order to escape blame for the violation

3.____

4. A certain police officer was patrolling a playground area where adolescent gangs had been causing troubles and holding drinking parties. He approached a teenage boy who was alone and drinking from a large paper cup. He asked the boy what he was drinking, and the boy replied *Coke*. The officer asked the boy for the cup, and the boy refused to give it to him. The officer then explained that he wanted to check the contents, and the boy still refused to give it to him. The officer then demanded the cup, and the boy reluctantly gave it to him. The officer smelled the contents of the cup and determined that it was, in fact, Coke. He then told the boy to move along and emptied the Coke on the ground.
Which one of the following is the MOST serious error, if any, made by the officer in handling this situation?
   A. The officer should not have made any effort to determine what was in the cup.
   B. The officer should not have explained to the boy why he wanted to have the cup.
   C. The officer should have returned the Coke to the boy and allowed the boy to stay where he was.
   D. The officer should have first placed the boy under arrest before taking the cup from him.
   E. None of the above since the officer made no error in handling the situation.

4.____

5. Sociological studies have revealed a great deal of information about the behavior and characteristics of homosexuals.
Which one of the following statements about male homosexuals is MOST accurate?
   A. Male homosexual activity is engaged in by less than 10% of the population.
   B. Most male homosexuals would like to be cured if it were possible.
   C. Male homosexuals are more likely than other sex deviates to commit assaults on female children.
   D. Most male homosexuals pose a threat to the morals and safety of a community and should be removed from the streets.

5.____

E. Most male homosexuals pose no threat to a community and are content to restrict their activities to people of similar tastes.

6. Which one of the following is the MOST important factor for the police department to consider in building a good public image?
   A. A good working relationship with the news media
   B. An efficient police-community relations program
   C. An efficient system for handling citizen complaints
   D. The proper maintenance of police facilities and equipment
   E. The behavior of individual officers in their contacts with the public

6._____

7. Following are four aspects of Black culture which sociologists and psychologists might possibly consider as health aspects:
   I. Use of hair straighteners   II. Use of skin bleaches
   III. Use of natural Afro hair styles   IV. Use of African style of dress
   Which one of the following MOST accurately classifies the above into those that sociologists do consider healthy and those that they do not?
   A. I and III are considered healthy, but II and IV are not
   B. I, III, and IV are considered healthy but II is not
   C. None of I, II, III, and IV is considered healthy
   D. III is considered healthy, but I, II, and IV are not
   E. III and IV are considered healthy, but I and II are not

7._____

8. Which one of the following situations is MOST responsible for making police-community relations more difficult in a densely populated, low income precinct?
   A. The majority of residents in such precincts do not want police on patrol in their communities.
   B. Radio patrol car sectors in such precincts are too small to give patrol officers an understanding of community problems
   C. The higher ratio of arrests per capita in such precincts leads law-abiding residents in such a precinct to feel oppressed by police.
   D. Such precincts tend to have little or no communication among residents so efforts to improve police-community relations must be on an individual level.
   E. This type of precinct has a higher rate of crime and, therefore, law-abiding residents are often bitter because they feel the police give them inferior protection.

8._____

9. Research studies based on having children draw pictures of police officers at work have shown that children of low income minority group parents are more likely to see police as aggressive than children of upper-middle class white parents. One police department had a group of low-income children participate in a 20-minute discussion with a police officer, and then allowed the youngsters a chance to sit in a police car, blow the siren, etc.
Which one of the following BEST states what effect, if any, this approach MOST likely had on the pictures drawn by the children when they were released two days later?
   A. The children showed almost no hostility toward police.
   B. The children showed significantly less hostility toward police.

9._____

C. The children showed significantly more hostility toward police.
D. There was essentially no change in the attitudes of the children.
E. The children showed a loss of respect for the police, who saw them as weak and permissive

10. Following are three possible complaints against police which might be made frequently by blacks living in cities where riots have taken place:
    I. Lack of adequate channels for complaints against police officers
    II. Failure of police departments to provide adequate protection for Blacks
    III. Discriminatory police employment or promotional practices with regard to Black officers

    Which one of the following choices MOST accurately classifies the above into those which have been frequent complaints and those which have not?
    A. I is a frequent complaint, but II and III are not.
    B. I and II are frequent complaints, but III is not.
    C. I and III are frequent complaints, but II is not.
    D. All of I, II, and III are frequent complaints.
    E. None of I, II, or III is a frequent complaint.

    10.____

11. A career criminal is one who actively engages in crime as his lifework. Which one of the following statements about *career criminals* is MOST accurate?
    A *career criminal*
    A. understands that prison is a normal occupational hazard
    B. is very likely to suffer from deep emotional and psychological problems
    C. has a lower average intelligence than the average for the general public
    D. is just as likely to engage in violence during a crime as any other criminal
    E. is less likely to have begun his crime career as a juvenile when compared to other criminals

    11.____

12. Which one of the following choices BEST describes the tactic of non-violent resistance as used by civil rights groups?
    The
    A. willingness of persons to accept unlawful arrest without resistance
    B. avoiding of prosecution for violations of law by refusing to appear in court when required
    C. teasing and verbal harassment of police officers in order to cause unlawful arrests
    D. intentional violation of a particular law by persons unwilling to accept the penalty for violating that law
    E. intentional violation of a particular law by persons willing to accept the penalty for violating that law

    12.____

13. Which one of the following is the MOST accurate statement about the civil disorders that occurred in the United States in the first nine months of 1967?
    A. Damage caused by riots was much greater than initial estimates indicated.
    B. They intended to be unplanned outbursts, not events planned by militants or agitators.

    13.____

C. The principal targets of attack were homes, schools, and businesses owned by Black merchants.
D. There were very few minor riots; either there were major riots or there were no riots.
E. The majority of persons killed or injured in the disorders were police officers and white civilians.

14. Some managers try to achieve goals by manipulating or deceiving subordinates into doing what the managers want. Such a manager normally is motivated by a desire to control people or by a desire to hide his own inadequacies. Such a manager also wants to hide the reasons for his actions from those he manages. This type of manager is often referred to as a *facade builder*. Which one of the following types of behavior is LEAST characteristic of this type of manager.
He
A. shows concern for other people
B. avoids criticizing other people
C. gives praise and approval easily
D. delegates responsibility for administering punishment
E. avoids getting involved in internal conflicts within the organization

14._____

15. Which one of the following choices states both the MOST PROBABLE effect on crime rate statistics of increased public confidence in police and also the MOST IMPORTANT reason for this effect?
A. The overall statistical crime rate would decrease because people would be less likely to commit crimes.
B. The overall statistical crime rate would increase because people would be more likely to report crimes.
C. The overall statistical crime rate would increase because police would probably be clearing more crimes by arrest.
D. The overall statistical crime rate would decrease because police would be less likely to arrest offender for minor violations.
E. Increased public confidence in police would have no effect on the overall statistical crime rate because this depends on the number of crimes committed, not public attitude toward police.

15._____

16. One of the important tasks of any administrator is the development of a proper filing system for classifying written documents by subject.
Following are three suggested rules for subject cross-referencing which might possibly be considered proper:
I. All filed material should have at least one subject cross-reference.
II. There should be no limit on the number of subject cross-references that may be made for a single record.
III. The original document should be filed under the primary classification subject, with only cross-reference sheets, not considered as records, being filed under the cross-reference subject classifications.

16._____

6 (#2)

Which one of the following choices MOST accurately classifies the above into those that are proper rules for cross-referencing and those that are not?
- A. I is a proper rule, but II and III are not.
- B. I and III are proper rules, but II is not.
- C. II and III are proper rules, but I is not
- D. III is a proper rule, but I and II are not.
- E. None of I, II, and III is a proper rule.

17. Wherever gambling, prostitution, and narcotics distribution openly flourish, they are usually accompanied by community charges of *protection* on the part of local police.
Which one of the following BEST states both whether or not such changes have merit and also the BEST reason therefor?
The charges
- A. *do not have, merit* because the nature of these operations makes them very difficult to detect
- B. *have merit*, because such operations cannot long continue openly without some measure of police protection
- C. *have merit*, because offenses of this type are among the easiest to eliminate
- D. *do not have merit*, because the local patrol forces probably do not have responsibility for large-scale vice enforcement
- E. *do not have merit*, because vice flourishes openly only in a community which desires it; therefore, it is the community that is providing the protection

17._____

18. The PRIMARY function of a department of social services is to
- A. refer needy persons to legally responsible relatives for support
- B. enable needy persons to become self-supporting
- C. refer ineligible persons to private agencies
- D. grant aid to needy eligible persons
- E. administer public assistance programs in which the federal and state governments do not participate

18._____

19. A public assistance program objective should be designed to
- A. provide for eligible persons in accordance with their individual requirements and with consideration of the circumstances in which they live
- B. provide for eligible persons at a standard of living equal to that enjoyed while they were self-supporting
- C. make sure that assistance payments from public funds are not too liberal
- D. guard against providing a better living for persons receiving aid than is enjoyed by the most frugal independent families
- E. eliminate the need for private welfare agencies

19._____

20. It is often stated that it would be better to abolish the need for relief rather than to extend the existing public assistance programs.

20._____

This statement suggests that
- A. existing legislation makes it too easy for people to apply for and receive assistance
- B. public assistance should be limited to institutional care for rehabilitative purposes
- C. the support of needy persons should be the responsibility of their own families and relatives rather than that of the government
- D. the existing criteria used to determine *need* for public assistance are too liberal and should be modified to include a *work test*
- E. attempts should be made to eradicate those forces in our social organization which cause poverty

21. The one of the following types of public assistance which is FREQUENTLY described as a *special privilege* is
    - A. veteran assistance
    - B. emergency assistance
    - C. aid to dependent children
    - D. old-age assistance
    - E. vocational rehabilitation of the handicapped

    21.____

22. The principle of *settlement* holds that each community is responsible for the care of its own members and that communities should not bear the costs of care for needy non-residents.
    This was an intrinsic principle of the
    - A. English Poor Laws
    - B. Home Rule Amendment
    - C. Single Tax Proposal
    - D. National Bankruptcy Regulations
    - E. Proportional Representation Act

    22.____

23. The FIRST form of state social security legislation developed in the United States was
    - A. health insurance
    - B. unemployment compensation
    - C. workmen's compensation
    - D. old-age insurance
    - E. old-age assistance

    23.____

24. The plan for establishing a federal government with Cabinet formerly called the Department of Health, Education, and Welfare was
    - A. vetoed by the President after having been passed by Congress
    - B. disapproved by the Senate after having been passed by the House of Representatives
    - C. rejected by both the Senate and the House of Representatives
    - D. enacted into legislation
    - E. determined to be unconstitutional

    24.____

25. Census Bureau reports show certain definite social trends in our population. One of these trends which was a MAJOR contributing factor in the establishment of the federal old-age insurance system is the
    - A. increased rate of immigration to the United States
    - B. rate at which the number of Americans living to 65 years of age and beyond is increasing

    25.____

C. increasing amounts spent for categorical relief in the country as a whole
D. decreasing number of legally responsible relatives who have been unable to assist he aged since the depression of 1929
E. number of states which have failed to meet their obligations in the care of the aged

---

KEY (CORRECT ANSWERS)

1.	E		11.	A
2.	B		12.	E
3.	A		13.	B
4.	C		14.	E
5.	E		15.	B
6.	E		16.	C
7.	E		17.	B
8.	E		18.	D
9.	B		19.	A
10.	D		20.	E

21. A
22. A
23. C
24. D
25. B

EXAMINATION SECTION
TEST 1

DIRECTIONS: Each question or incomplete statement is followed by several suggested answers or completions. Select the one that BEST answers the question or completes the statement. *PRINT THE LETTER OF IN THE CORRECT ANSWER THE SPACE AT THE RIGHT.*

1. Reports show that more men than women are physically handicapped MAINLY because   1._____

   A. women are instinctively more cautious than men
   B. men are more likely to have congenital deformities
   C. women tend to seek surgical remedies because of greater concern over personal appearance
   D. men have lower ability to recover from injury
   E. men are more likely to be exposed to hazardous conditions

2. Of the following, the explanation married women give MOST frequently for seeking employment outside the home is that they wish to   2._____

   A. escape the drudgeries of home life
   B. develop secondary employment skills
   C. maintain an emotionally satisfying career
   D. provide the main support for the family
   E. supplement the family income

3. Of the following home conditions, the one *most likely* to cause emotional disturbances in children is   3._____

   A. increased birthrate following the war
   B. disrupted family relationships
   C. lower family income than that of neighbors
   D. higher family income than that of neighbors
   E. overcrowded living conditions

4. Casual unemployment, as distinguished from other types of unemployment, is traceable MOST readily to   4._____

   A. a decrease in the demand for labor as a result of scientific progress
   B. more or less haphazard changes in the demand for labor in certain industries
   C. periodic changes in the demand for labor in certain industries
   D. disturbances and disruptions in industry resulting from international trade barriers
   E. increased mobility of the population

5. Labor legislation, although primarily intended for the benefit of the employee, MAY aid the employer by   5._____

   A. increasing his control over the immediate labor market
   B. prohibiting government interference with operating policies
   C. protecting him, through equalization of labor costs, from being undercut by other employers
   D. transferring to the general taxpayer the principal costs of industrial hazards of accident and unemployment
   E. increasing the pensions of civil service employees

6. When employment and unemployment figures both decline, the MOST probable conclusion is that

   A. the population has reached a condition of equilibrium
   B. seasonal employment has ended
   C. the labor force has decreased
   D. payments for unemployment insurance have been increased
   E. industrial progress has reduced working hours

7. An individual with an I.Q. of 100 may be said to have demonstrated _____ intelligence.

   A. superior
   B. absolute
   C. substandard
   D. approximately average
   E. high average

8. While state legislatures differ in many respects, all of them are *most nearly* alike in

   A. provisions for retirement of members
   B. rate of pay
   C. length of legislative sessions
   D. method of selection of their members
   E. length of term of office

9. If a state passed a law in a field under Congressional jurisdiction and if Congress subsequently passed contrary legislation, the state provision would be

   A. regarded as never having existed
   B. valid until the next session of the state legislature, which would be obliged to repeal it
   C. superseded by the federal statute
   D. ratified by Congress
   E. still operative in the state involved

10. Power to pardon offenses committed against the people of the United States is vested in the

    A. Supreme Court of the United States
    B. United States District Courts
    C. Federal Bureau of Investigation
    D. United States Parole Board
    E. President of the United States

11. As distinguished from formal social control of an individual's behavior, an example of informal social control is that exerted by

    A. public opinion
    B. religious doctrine
    C. educational institutions
    D. statutes
    E. public health measures

12. The PRINCIPAL function of the jury in a jury trial is to decide questions of

    A. equity
    B. fact
    C. injunction
    D. contract
    E. law

13. Of the following rights of an individual, the one which usually depends on citizenship as distinguished from those given anyone living under the laws of the United States is the right to

    A. receive public assistance
    B. hold an elective office
    C. petition the government for redress of grievances
    D. receive equal protection of the laws
    E. be accorded a trial by jury

14. If the characteristics of a person were being studied by competent observers, it would be expected that their observations would differ MOST markedly with respect to their evaluation of the person's

    A. intelligence
    B. nutritional condition
    C. temperamental characteristics
    D. weight
    E. height

15. If there are evidences of dietary deficiency in families where cereals make up a major portion of the diet, the *most likely* reason for this deficiency is that

    A. cereals cause absorption of excessive quantities of water
    B. persons who concentrate their diet on cereals do not chew their food properly
    C. carbohydrates are deleterious
    D. other essential food elements are omitted
    E. children eat cereals too rapidly

16. Although malnutrition is generally associated with poverty, dietary studies of population groups in the United States reveal that

    A. malnutrition is most often due to a deficiency of nutrients found chiefly in high-cost foods
    B. there has been overemphasis of the casual relationship between poverty and malnutrition
    C. malnutrition is found among people with sufficient money to be well fed
    D. a majority of the population in all income groups is undernourished
    E. malnutrition is not a factor in the incidence of rickets

17. The organization which has as one of its primary functions the mitigation of suffering caused by famine, fire, floods, and other national calamities is the

    A. National Safety Council
    B. Salvation Army
    C. Public Administration Service
    D. American National Red Cross
    E. American Legion

18. The MAIN difference between public welfare and private social agencies is that in public agencies,

    A. case records are open to the public
    B. the granting of assistance cannot be sufficiently flexible to meet the varying needs of individual recipients
    C. only financial assistance may be provided
    D. all policies and procedures must be based upon statutory authorizations
    E. economical and efficient administration are stressed because their funds are obtained through public taxation

19. A recipient of relief who is in need of the services of an attorney but is unable to pay the customary fees, should *generally* be referred to the

    A. Small Claims Court
    B. Domestic Relations Court
    C. County Lawyers Association
    D. City Law Department
    E. Legal Aid Society

20. An injured workman should file his claim for workmen's compensation with the

    A. State Labor Relations Board
    B. Division of Placement and Unemployment Insurance
    C. State Industrial Commission
    D. Workmen's Compensation Board
    E. State Insurance Board

21. The type of insurance found MOST frequently among families such as those assisted by the Department of Social Services is

    A. accident   B. straight life
    C. endowment   D. industrial
    E. personal liability

22. Of the following items in the standard budget of the Department of Social Services, the one for which actual expenditures would be MOST constant throughout the year is

    A. fuel   B. housing
    C. medical care   D. clothing
    E. household replacements

23. The MOST frequent cause of "broken homes" is attributed to the

    A. temperamental incompatibilities of parents and in-laws
    B. extension of the system of children's courts
    C. psychopathic irresponsibility of the parents
    D. institutionalization of one of the spouses
    E. death of one or both spouses

24. In rearing children, the problems of the widower are usually greater than those of the widow, largely because of the

   A. tendency of widowers to impose excessively rigid moral standards
   B. increased economic hardship
   C. added difficulty of maintaining a desirable home
   D. possibility that a stepmother will be added to the household
   E. prevalent masculine prejudice against pursuits which are inherently feminine

25. Foster-home placement of children is often advocated in preference to institutionalization *primarily* because

   A. the law does not provide for local supervision of children's institutions
   B. institutions furnish a more expensive type of care
   C. the number of institutions is insufficient compared to the number of children needing care
   D. children are not well treated in institutions
   E. foster homes provide a more normal environment for children

KEY (CORRECT ANSWERS)

1. E	11. A
2. E	12. B
3. B	13. B
4. B	14. C
5. C	15. D
6. C	16. C
7. D	17. D
8. D	18. D
9. C	19. E
10. E	20. D

21. D
22. B
23. E
24. C
25. E

TEST 2

DIRECTIONS: Each question or incomplete statement is followed by several suggested answers or completions. Select the one that BEST answers the question or completes the statement. *PRINT THE LETTER OF THE CORRECT ANSWER IN THE SPACE AT THE RIGHT.*

1. Of the following, the category MOST likely to yield the greatest reduction in cost to the taxpayer under improved employment conditions is

    A. home relief, including aid to the homeless
    B. aid to the blind
    C. aid to dependent children
    D. old-age assistance

2. One of the MOST common characteristics of the chronic alcoholic is

    A. low intelligence level
    B. wanderlust
    C. psychosis
    D. egocentricity

3. Of the following factors leading toward the cure of the alcoholic, the MOST important is thought to be

    A. removal of all alcohol from the immediate environment
    B. development of a sense of personal adequacy
    C. social disapproval of drinking
    D. segregation from former companions

4. The Federal Housing Administration is the agency which

    A. insures mortgages made by lending institutions for new construction or remodeling of old construction
    B. provides federal aid for state and local government for slum clearance and housing for very low income families
    C. subsidizes the building industry through direct grants
    D. provides for the construction of low-cost housing projects owned and operated by the federal government

5. In comparing the advantages of foster home over institutional placement, it is generally agreed that institutional care is LEAST advisable for children

    A. who cannot sustain the intimacy of foster family living because of their experiences with their own parents
    B. who are socially well-adjusted or have had considerable experience in living with a family
    C. who have need for special facilities for observation, diagnosis, and treatment
    D. whose natural parents find it difficult to accept the idea of foster home placement because of its close resemblance to adoption

6. The school can play a vital part in detecting the child who displays overt symptomatic behavior indicative of social maladjustment CHIEFLY because the teacher has the opportunity to

   A. assume a pseudo-parental role in regard to discipline and punishment, thereby limiting the extent of the maladjusted child's anti-social behavior
   B. observe how the child relates to the group and what reactions are stimulated in him by his peer relationships
   C. determine whether the adjustment difficulties displayed by the child were brought on by the teacher herself or by the other students
   D. help the child's parents to resolve the difficulties in adjustment which are indicated by the child's reactions to the social pressures exerted by his peers

6._____

7. In treating juvenile delinquents, it has been found that there are some who make better social adjustment through group treatment than through an individual casework approach.
   In selecting delinquent boys for group treatment, the one of the following which is the MOST important consideration is that

   A. the boys to be treated in one group be friends or from the same community
   B. only boys who consent to group treatment be included in the group
   C. the ages of the boys included in the group vary as much as possible
   D. only boys who have not reacted to an individual casework approach be included in the group

7._____

8. Multi-problem families are generally characterized by various functional indicators.
   Of the following, the family which is *most likely* to be a multi-problem family is one which has

   A. unemployed adult family members
   B. parents with diagnosed character disorders
   C. children and parents with a series of difficulties in the community
   D. poor housekeeping standards

8._____

9. Multi-problem families generally have a complex history of intervention by a variety of social agencies.
   Of the following phases involved in planning for their treatment, the one which is MOST important to consider FIRST is the

   A. joint decision to limit any help to be given
   B. analysis of facts and definition of the problems involved
   C. determination of treatment priorities
   D. study of available community resources

9._____

10. The development of good public relations in the area for which the supervisor is responsible should be considered by the supervisor as

    A. not his responsibility as he is primarily responsible for his workers' services
    B. dependent upon him as he is in the best position to interpret the department to the community
    C. not important to the adequate functioning of the department
    D. a part of his method of carrying out his job responsibility as what his workers do affects the community

11. Of the following, the LEAST accurate statement concerning the relationship of public and private social agencies is that

    A. both have an important and necessary function to perform
    B. they are not to be considered as competing or rival agencies
    C. they are cooperating agencies
    D. their work is based on fundamentally different social work concepts

12. Of the following, the LEAST accurate statement concerning the worker-client relationship is that the worker should have the ability to

    A. express warmth of feeling in appropriate ways as a basis for a professional relationship which creates confidence
    B. feel appropriately in the relationship without losing the ability to see the situation in the perspective necessary to help the people immersed in it
    C. identify himself with the client so that the worker's personality does not influence the client
    D. use keen observation and perceive what is significant with a new range of appreciation of the meaning of the situation to the client

13. Of the following, the MOST fundamental psychological concept underlying case work in the public assistance field is that

    A. eligibility for public assistance should be reviewed from time to time
    B. workers should be aware of the prevalence of psychological disabilities among members of families on public assistance
    C. workers should realize the necessity of carrying out the policies laid down by the state office in order that state aid may be received
    D. in the process of receiving assistance, recipients should not be deprived of their normal status of self-direction

14. Of the following, the MOST comprehensive as well as the MOST accurate statement concerning the professional attitude of the social worker is that he should

    A. have a real concern for, and an intelligent interest in, the welfare of the client
    B. recognize that the client's feelings rather than the realities of his needs are of major importance to the client
    C. put at the client's service the worker's knowledge and sincere interest in him
    D. use his insight and understanding to make sound decisions about the client

15. The one of the following reasons for refusing a job which is LEAST acceptable, from the viewpoint of maintaining a client's continued rights to unemployment insurance benefits, is that

    A. acceptance of the job would interfere with the client's joining or retaining membership in a labor union
    B. there is a strike, lockout, or other industrial controversy in the establishment where employment is offered
    C. the distance from the place of employment to his home is greater than seems justified to the client
    D. the wages offered are lower than the prevailing wages in that locality

16. Experience pragmatically suggests that dislocation from cultural roots and customs makes for tension, insecurity, and anxiety. This holds for the child as well as the adolescent, for the new immigrant as well as the second-generation citizen.
    Of the following, the MOST important implication of the above statement for a social worker in any setting is that

    A. anxiety, distress, and incapacity are always personal and can be understood best only through an understanding of the child's present cultural environment
    B. in order to resolve the conflicts caused by the displacement of a child from a home with one cultural background to one with another, it is essential that the child fully replace his old culture with the new one
    C. no treatment goal can be envisaged for a dislocated child which does not involve a value judgment which is itself culturally determined
    D. anxiety and distress result from a child's reaction to culturally oriented treatment goals

17. Accepting the fact that mentally gifted children represent superior heredity, the United States faces an important eugenic problem CHIEFLY because

    A. unless these mentally gifted children mature and reproduce more rapidly than the less intelligent children, the nation is heading for a lowering of the average intelligence of its people
    B. although the mentally gifted child always excels scholastically, he generally has less physical stamina than the normal child and tends to lower the nation's population physically
    C. the mentally subnormal are increasing more rapidly than the mentally gifted in America, thus affecting the overall level of achievement of the gifted child
    D. unless the mental level of the general population is raised to that of the gifted child, the mentally gifted will eventually usurp the reigns of government and dominate the mentally weaker

18. The form of psychiatric treatment which requires the LEAST amount of participation on the part of the patient is

    A. psychoanalysis
    B. psychotherapy
    C. shock therapy
    D. non-directive therapy

19. Tests administered by psychologists for the PRIMARY purpose of measuring intelligence are known as _____ tests.

    A. projective
    B. validating
    C. psychometric
    D. apperception

20. In recent years, there have been some significant changes in the treatment of patients in state psychiatric hospitals. These changes are PRIMARILY caused by the use of

    A. electric shock therapy
    B. tranquilizing drugs
    C. steroids
    D. the open-ward policy

21. The psychological test which makes use of a set of twenty pictures, each depicting a dramatic scene, is known as the

    A. Goodenough Test
    B. Thematic Apperception Test
    C. Minnesota Multiphasic Personality Inventory
    D. Healy Picture Completion Test

22. One of the MOST effective ways in which experimental psychologists have been able to study the effects on personality of heredity and environment has been through the study of

    A. primitive cultures
    B. identical twins
    C. mental defectives
    D. newborn infants

23. In hospitals with psychiatric divisions, the psychiatric function is PREDOMINANTLY that of

    A. the training of personnel in all psychiatric disciplines
    B. protection of the community against potentially dangerous psychiatric patients
    C. research and study of psychiatric patients so that new knowledge and information can be made generally available
    D. short-term hospitalization designed to determine diagnosis and recommendations for treatment

24. Predictions of human behavior on the basis of past behavior frequently are INACCURATE because

    A. basic patterns of human behavior are in a continual state of flux
    B. human behavior is not susceptible to explanation of a scientific nature
    C. the underlying psychological mechanisms of behavior are not completely understood
    D. quantitative techniques for the measurement of stimuli and responses are unavailable

25. Socio-cultural factors are being re-evaluated in casework practice as they influence both the worker and the client in their participation in the casework process.
Of the following factors, the one which is currently being studied MOST widely is the

25._____

   A. social class of worker and client and its significance in casework
   B. difference in native intelligence which can be ascribed to racial origin of an individual
   C. cultural values affecting the areas in which an individual functions
   D. necessity in casework treatment of the client's membership in an organized religious group

---

KEY (CORRECT ANSWERS)

1.	A	11.	D
2.	D	12.	C
3.	B	13.	D
4.	A	14.	C
5.	B	15.	C
6.	B	16.	C
7.	B	17.	A
8.	C	18.	C
9.	B	19.	C
10.	D	20.	B

21. B
22. B
23. D
24. C
25. C

EXAMINATION SECTION
TEST 1

DIRECTIONS: Each question or incomplete statement is followed by several suggested answers or completions. Select the one that BEST answers the question or completes the statement. *PRINT THE LETTER OF THE CORRECT ANSWER IN THE SPACE AT THE RIGHT.*

1. Deviant behavior is a sociological term used to describe behavior which is not in accord with generally accepted standards. This may include juvenile delinquency, adult criminality, mental or physical illness.
   Comparison of normal with deviant behavior is useful to social workers because it

   A. makes it possible to establish watertight behavioral descriptions
   B. provides evidence of differential social behavior which distinguishes deviant from normal behavior
   C. indicates that deviant behavior is of no concern to social workers
   D. provides no evidence that social role is a determinant of behavior

   1.____

2. Alcoholism may affect an individual client's ability to function as a spouse, parent, worker, and citizen.
   A social worker's MAIN responsibility to a client with a history of alcoholism is to

   A. interpret to the client the causes of alcoholism as a disease syndrome
   B. work with the alcoholic's family to accept him as he is and stop trying to reform him
   C. encourage the family of the alcoholic to accept casework treatment
   D. determine the origins of his particular drinking problem, establish a diagnosis, and work out a treatment plan for him

   2.____

3. There is a trend to regard narcotic addiction as a form of illness for which the current methods of intervention have not been effective.
   Research on the combination of social, psychological, and physical causes of addiction would indicate that social workers should

   A. oppose hospitalization of addicts in institutions
   B. encourage the addict to live normally at home
   C. recognize that there is no successful treatment for addiction and act accordingly
   D. use the existing community facilities differentially for each addict

   3.____

4. A study of social relationships among delinquent and non-delinquent youth has shown that

   A. delinquent youth generally conceal their true feelings and maintain furtive social contacts
   B. delinquents are more impulsive and vivacious than law-abiding boys
   C. non-delinquent youths diminish their active social relationships in order to sublimate any anti-social impulses
   D. delinquent and non-delinquent youths exhibit similar characteristics of impulsiveness and vivaciousness

   4.____

5. The one of the following which is the CHIEF danger of interpreting the delinquent behavior of a child in terms of morality *alone* when attempting to get at its causes is that

   A. this tends to overlook the likelihood that the causes of the child's actions are more than a negation of morality and involve varied symptoms of disturbance
   B. a child's moral outlook toward life and society is largely colored by that of his parents, thus encouraging parent-child conflict
   C. too careful a consideration of the moral aspects of the offense and of the child's needs may often negate the demands of justice in a case
   D. standards of morality may be of no concern to the delinquent and he may not realize the seriousness of his offenses

6. Experts in the field of personnel administration are generally agreed that an employee should not be under the immediate supervision of more than one supervisor. A certain worker, because of an emergency situation, divides his time equally between two limited caseloads on a prearranged time schedule. Each unit has a different supervisor, and the worker performs substantially the same duties in each caseload.
   The above statement is pertinent in this situation CHIEFLY because

   A. each supervisor, feeling that the cases in her unit should have priority, may demand too much of the worker's time
   B. the two supervisors may have different standards of work performance and may prefer different methods of doing the work
   C. the worker works part-time on each caseload and may not have full knowledge or control of the situation in either caseload
   D. the task of evaluating the worker's services will be doubled, with two supervisors instead of one having to rate his work

7. Experts in modern personnel management generally agree that employees on all job levels should be permitted to offer suggestions for improving work methods.
   Of the following, the CHIEF limitation of such suggestions is that they may, at times,

   A. be offered primarily for financial reward and not show genuine interest in improvement of work methods
   B. be directed towards making individual jobs easier
   C. be restricted by the employees' fear of radically changing the work methods favored by their supervisors
   D. show little awareness of the effects on the overall objectives and functions of the entire agency

8. Through the supervisory process and relationship, the supervisor is trying to help workers gain increased self-awareness.
   Of the following statements concerning this process, the one which is MOST accurate is:

   A. Self-awareness is developed gradually so that worker can learn to control his own reactions.
   B. Worker is expected to be introspective primarily for his own enlightenment.
   C. Supervisor is trying to help worker handle any emotional difficulties he may reveal.
   D. Worker is expected at the onset to share and determine with the supervisor what in his previous background makes it difficult for him to use certain ideas.

9. The one of the following statements concerning principles in the learning process which is LEAST accurate is:

   A. Some degree of regression on the part of the worker is usually natural in the process of development and this should be accepted by the supervisor.
   B. When a beginning worker shows problems, the supervisor should first handle this behavior as a personality difficulty.
   C. It has been found in the work training process that some degree of resistance is usually inevitable.
   D. The emotional content of work practice may tend to set up *blind spots* in workers.

10. Of the following, the one that represents the BEST basis for planning the content of a successful staff development program is the

    A. time available for meetings
    B. chief social problems of the community
    C. common needs of the staff workers as related to the situations with which they are dealing
    D. experimental programs conducted by other agencies

11. In planning staff development seminars, the MOST valuable topics for discussion are likely to be those selected from

    A. staff suggestions based on the staff's interest and needs
    B. topics recommended for consideration by professional organizations
    C. topics selected by the administration based on demonstrated limitations of staff skill and knowledge
    D. topics selected by the administration based on a combination of staff interest and objectivity evaluated staff needs

12. Staff meetings designed to promote professional staff development are MOST likely to achieve this goal when

    A. there is the widest participation among all staff members who attend the meetings
    B. participation by the most skilled and experienced staff members is predominant
    C. participation by selected staff members is planned before the meeting sessions
    D. supervisory personnel take major responsibility for participation

13. Assume that you are the leader of a conference attended by representatives of various city and private agencies. After the conference has been underway for a considerable time, you realize that the representative of one of these agencies has said nothing.
    It would generally be BEST for you to

    A. ask him if he would like to say anything
    B. ask the group a pertinent question that he would probably be best able to answer
    C. make no special effort to include him in the conversation
    D. address the next question you planned to ask to him directly

14. A member of a decision-making conference generally makes his BEST contribution to the conference when he

    A. compromises on his own point of view and accepts most of the points of other conference members
    B. persuades the conference to accept all or most of his points

C. persuades the conference to accept his major proposals but will yield on the minor ones
D. succeeds in integrating his ideas with the ideas of the other conference members

15. Of the following, the LEAST accurate statement concerning the compilation and use of statistics in administration is:

   A. Interpretation of statistics is as necessary as their compilation.
   B. Statistical records of expenditures and services are one of the bases for budget preparation.
   C. Statistics on the quality of services rendered to the community will clearly delineate the human values achieved.
   D. The results achieved from collecting and compiling statistics must be in keeping with the cost and effort required.

16. An important administrative problem is how precisely to define the limits on authority that is delegated to subordinate supervisors.
    Such definition of limits of authority SHOULD be

   A. as precise as possible and practicable in all areas
   B. as precise as possible and practicable in all areas of function, but should allow considerable flexibility in the area of personnel management
   C. as precise as possible and practicable in the area of personnel management, but should allow considerable flexibility in the areas of function
   D. in general terms so as to allow considerable flexibility both in the areas of function and in the areas of personnel management

17. The LEAST important of the following reasons why a particular activity should be assigned to a unit which performs activities dissimilar to it is that

   A. close coordination is needed between the particular activity and other activities performed by the unit
   B. it will enhance the reputation and prestige of the unit supervisor
   C. the unit makes frequent use of the results of this particular activity
   D. the unit supervisor has a sound knowledge and understanding of the particular activity

18. The MOST important of the following reasons why the average resident of a deteriorated slum neighborhood resists relocation to an area in the suburbs with better physical accommodations is that he

   A. does not recognize as undesirable the characteristics which are responsible for deterioration of the neighborhood
   B. has some expectation of neighborly assistance in his old home in times of stress and adversity
   C. hopes for better days when he may be able to become a figure of some importance and envy in the old neighborhood
   D. is attuned to the noise of the city and fears the quiet of the suburb

19. From a psychological and sociological point of view, the MOST important of the following dangers to the persons living in an economically depressed area in which the only step taken by governmental and private social agencies to assist these persons is the granting of a dole is that

   A. industry will be reluctant to expand its operations in that area
   B. the dole will encourage additional non-producers to enter the area
   C. the residents of the area will probably have to find their own solution to their problems
   D. their permanent dependency will be fostered

20. The term *real wages* is GENERALLY used by economists to mean the

   A. amount of take-home pay left after taxes, social security, and other such deductions have been made by the employer
   B. average wage actually earned during a calendar or fiscal year
   C. family income expressed on a per capita basis
   D. wages expressed in terms of its buyer power

21. It has, at times, been suggested that an effective way to eradicate juvenile delinquency would be to arrest and punish the parents for the criminal actions of their delinquent children.
   The one of the following which is the CHIEF defect of this proposal is that

   A. it fails to get at the cause of the delinquent act and tends to further weaken disturbed parent-child relationships
   B. since the criminally inclined child has apparently demonstrated little love or affection for his parent, the child will be unlikely to amend his behavior in order to avoid hurting his parent
   C. the child who commits anti-social acts does so in many cases in order to hurt his parents so that this proposal would not only increase the parents' sorrow, but would also serve as an incentive to more delinquency by the child
   D. the punishment should be limited to the person who commits the illegal action rather than to those who are most interested in his welfare

22. Surveys which have compared the relative stability of marriages between white persons with marriages between non-white persons in this country have shown that, among Blacks, there is

   A. a significantly higher percentage of spouses absent from the household than among whites
   B. a significantly higher percentage of spouses absent from the household than among whites living in the South, but the opposite is true in the Northeast
   C. a significantly lower percentage of spouses absent from the household than among whites
   D. no significant difference in the percentage of spouses absent from the household when compared with the white population

23. A phenomenon found in the cultural and recreational patterns of European immigrant families in America is that, generally, the foreign-born adults

   A. as well as their children, tend soon to forget their old-world activities and adopt the cultural and recreational customs of America
   B. as well as their children, tend to retain and continue their old-world cultural and recreational pursuits, and find it equally difficult to adopt those of America
   C. tend soon to drop their old pursuits and adopt the cultural and recreational patterns of America while their children find it somewhat more difficult to make this change
   D. tend to retain and continue their old-world cultural and recreational pursuits while their children tend to rapidly replace these by the games and cultural patterns of America

23.___

24. Certain mores of migrant groups are strengthened under the impact of their contact with the native society while other mores are weakened.
In the case of Puerto Ricans who have come to the city, the effect of such contact upon their traditional family structure has been a

   A. strengthening of the former maternalistic family structure
   B. strengthening of the former paternalistic family structure
   C. weakening of the former maternalistic family structure
   D. weakening of the former paternalistic family structure

24.___

25. Administrative reviews and special studies of independent experts, as reported by the Department of Health, Education and Welfare, indicate that the proportion of recipients of public assistance who receive such assistance through *wilful misrepresentation* of the facts is

   A. less than 1%
   B. about 4%
   C. between 4% and 7%
   D. between 7% and 10%

25.___

KEY (CORRECT ANSWERS)

1. B
2. D
3. D
4. B
5. A

6. B
7. D
8. A
9. B
10. C

11. D
12. A
13. B
14. D
15. C

16. A
17. B
18. B
19. D
20. D

21. A
22. A
23. D
24. D
25. A

TEST 2

DIRECTIONS: Each question or incomplete statement is followed by several suggested answers or completions. Select the one that BEST answers the question or completes the statement. *PRINT THE LETTER OF THE CORRECT ANSWER IN THE SPACE AT THE RIGHT.*

1. In order to meet more adequately the public assistance needs occasioned by sudden changes in the national economy, social service agencies, in general, recommend, as a matter of preference, that

    A. each locality build up reserve funds to care for needy unemployed persons in order to avoid a breakdown of local resources such as occurred during the depression
    B. the federal government assume total responsibility for the administration of public assistance
    C. state settlement laws be strictly enforced so that unemployed workers will be encouraged to move from the emergency industry centers to their former homes
    D. a federal-state-local program of general assistance be established with need as the only eligibility requirement
    E. eligibility requirements be tightened to assure that only legitimately worthy local residents receive the available assistance

    1.____

2. The MOST practical method of maintaining income for the majority of aged persons who are no longer able to work, or for the families of those workers who are deceased, is a(n)

    A. comprehensive system of non-categorical assistance on a basis of cash payments
    B. integrated system of public assistance and extensive work relief programs
    C. co-ordinated system of providing care in institutions and foster homes
    D. system of contributory insurance in which a cash benefit is paid as a matter of right
    E. expanded system of diagnostic and treatment centers

    2.____

3. With the establishment of insurance and assistance programs under the Social Security Act, many institutional programs for the aged have tended to the greatest extent toward an increased emphasis on providing, of the following types of assistance,

    A. care for the aged by denominational groups
    B. care for children requiring institutional treatment
    C. recreational facilities for the able-bodied aged
    D. training facilities in industrial homework for the aged
    E. care for the chronically ill and infirm aged

    3.____

4. Of the following terms, the one which BEST describes the Social Security Act is

    A. enabling legislation
    B. regulatory statute
    C. appropriations act
    D. act of mandamus
    E. provisional enactment

    4.____

5. Of the following, the term which MOST accurately describes an appropriation is 5.___

   A. authority to spend
   B. itemized estimate
   C. *fund* accounting
   D. anticipated expenditure
   E. executive budget

6. When business expansion causes a demand for labor, the worker group which benefits MOST immediately is the group comprising 6.___

   A. employed workers
   B. inexperienced workers under 21 years of age
   C. experienced workers 21 to 25 years of age
   D. inexperienced older workers
   E. experienced workers over 40 years of age

7. The MOST important failure in our present system of providing social work services in local communities is the 7.___

   A. absence of adequate facilities for treating mental illness
   B. lack of coordination of available data and service in the community
   C. poor quality of the casework services provided by the public agencies
   D. limitations of the probation and parole services
   E. inadequacy of private family welfare services

8. Recent studies of the relationship between incidence of illness and the use of available treatment services among various population groups in the United States show that 8.___

   A. while lower-income families use medical services with greater frequency, total expenditures are greater among the upper-income groups
   B. although the average duration of a period of medical care increases with increasing income, the average frequency of obtaining care decreases with increasing income
   C. adequacy of medical service is inversely related to frequency of illness and size of family income
   D. families in the higher-income brackets have a heavier incidence of illness and make greater use of medical services than do those in the lower-income brackets
   E. both as to frequency and duration, the distribution of illness falls equally on all groups, but the use of medical services increases with income

9. The category of disease which most public health departments and authorities usually are NOT equipped to handle *directly* is that of 9.___

   A. chronic disease
   B. bronchial disturbances
   C. venereal disease
   D. mosquito-borne diseases
   E. incipient forms of tuberculosis

3 (#2)

10. Recent statistical analyses of the causes of death in the United States indicate that medical science has now reached the stage where it would be preferable to increase its research toward control, among the following, PRINCIPALLY of

    A. accidents
    B. suicides
    C. communicable disease
    D. chronic disease
    E. infant mortality

10.____

11. Although the distinction between mental disease and mental deficiency is fairly definite, both these conditions USUALLY represent

    A. diseases of one part or organ of the body rather than of the whole person
    B. an inadequacy existing from birth or shortly afterwards and appearing as a simplicity of intelligence
    C. a deficiency developing later in life and characterized by distortions of attitude and belief
    D. inadequacies in meeting life situations and in conducting one's affairs
    E. somewhat transitory conditions characterized by disturbances of consciousness

11.____

12. According to studies made by reliable medical research organizations in the United States, differences among the states in proportion of physicians to population are MOST directly related to the

    A. geographic resources among the states
    B. skill of the physicians
    C. relative proportions of urban and rural people in the population of the states
    D. number of specialists in the ranks of the physicians
    E. health status of the people in the various states

12.____

13. One of the MAIN advantages of incorporating a charitable organization is that

    A. gifts or property of a corporation cannot be held in perpetuity
    B. gifts to unincorporated charitable organizations are not deductible from the taxable income
    C. incorporation gives less legal standing or *personality* than an informal partnership
    D. members of a corporation cannot be held liable for debts contracted by the organization
    E. a corporate organization cannot be sued

13.____

14. The BASIC principle underlying a social security program is that the government should provide

    A. aid to families that is not dependent on state or local participation
    B. assistance to any worthy family unable to maintain itself independently
    C. protection to individuals against some of the social risks that are inherent in an industrialized society
    D. safeguards against those factors leading to economic depression

14.____

35

15. The activities of state and local public welfare agencies are dependent to a large degree on the public assistance program of the federal government.
The one of the following which the federal government has NOT been successful in achieving within the local agencies is the

    A. broadening of the scope of public assistance administration
    B. expansion of the categorical programs
    C. improvement of the quality of service given to clients
    D. standardization of the administration of general assistance programs

16. Of the following statements, the one which BEST describes the federal government's position, as stated in the Social Security Act, with regard to tests of character or fitness to be administered by local or state welfare departments to prospective clients is that

    A. no tests of character are required but they are not specifically prohibited
    B. if tests of character are used, they must be uniform throughout the state
    C. tests of character are contrary to the philosophy of the federal government and are to be considered illegal
    D. no tests of character are required, and assistance to those states that use them will be withheld

17. An increase in the size of the welfare grant may increase the cost of the welfare program not only in terms of those already on the welfare rolls, but because it may result in an increase in the number of people on the rolls.
The CHIEF reason that an increase in the size of the grant may cause an increase in the number of people on the rolls is that the increased grant may

    A. induce low-salaried wage earners to apply for assistance rather than continue at their menial jobs
    B. make eligible for assistance many people whose resources are just above the previous standard
    C. induce many people to apply for assistance who hesitated to do so because of meagerness of the previous grant
    D. make relatives less willing to contribute because the welfare grant can more adequately cover their dependents' needs

18. One of the MAIN differences between the use of casework methods by a public welfare agency and by a private welfare agency is that the public welfare agency

    A. requires that the applicant be eligible for the services it offers
    B. cannot maintain a non-judgmental attitude toward its clients because of legal requirements
    C. places less emphasis on efforts to change the behavior of its clients
    D. must be more objective in its approach to the client because public funds are involved

19. All definitions of social casework include certain major assumptions.
Of the following, the one which is NOT considered a major assumption is that

    A. the individual and society are interdependent
    B. social forces influence behavior and attitudes, affording opportunity for self-development and contribution to the world in which we live
    C. reconstruction of the total personality and reorganization of the total environment are specific goals
    D. the client is a responsible participant at every step in the solution of his problems

20. In order to provide those services to problem families which will help restore them to a self-maintaining status, it is necessary to FIRST

   A. develop specific plans to meet the individual needs of the problem family
   B. reduce the size of those caseloads composed of multi-problem families
   C. remove them from their environment and provide them with the means of overcoming their dependency
   D. identify the factors causing their dependency and creating problems for them

21. Of the following, the type of service which can provide the client with the MOST enduring help is that service which

   A. provides him with material aid and relieves the stress of his personal problems
   B. assists him to do as much as he can for himself and leaves him free to make his own decisions
   C. directs his efforts towards returning to a self-maintaining status and provides him with desirable goals
   D. gives him the feeling that the agency is interested in him as an individual and stands ready to assist him with his problems

22. Psychiatric interpretation of unconscious motivations can bring childhood conflicts into the framework of adult understanding and open the way for them to be resolved, but the interpretation must come from within the client.
    This statement means MOST NEARLY that

   A. treatment is merely diagnosis in reverse
   B. explaining a client to himself will lead to the resolution of his problems
   C. the client must arrive at an understanding of his problems
   D. unresolved childhood conflicts create problems for the adult

23. A significant factor in the United States economic picture is the state of the labor market. Of the following, the MOST important development affecting the labor market has been

   A. an expansion of the national defense effort creating new plant capacity
   B. the general increase in personal income as a result of an increase in overtime pay in manufacturing industries
   C. the growth of manufacturing as a result of automation
   D. a demand for a large number of jobs resulting from new job applicants as well as from displacement of workers by automation

24. A typical characteristic of the United States population over 65 is that MOST of them

   A. are independent and capable of self-support
   B. live in their own homes but require various supportive services
   C. live in institutions for the aged
   D. require constant medical attention at home or in an institution

25. The one of the following factors which is MOST important in preventing persons 65 years of age and older from getting employment is the

   A. misconceptions by employers of skills and abilities of senior citizens
   B. lack of skill in modern industrial techniques of persons in this age group
   C. social security laws restricting employment of persons in this age group
   D. unwillingness of persons in this age group to continue supporting themselves

KEY (CORRECT ANSWERS)

1. D
2. D
3. E
4. A
5. A

6. B
7. B
8. C
9. A
10. D

11. D
12. C
13. D
14. C
15. D

16. A
17. B
18. C
19. C
20. D

21. B
22. C
23. D
24. B
25. A

EXAMINATION SECTION
TEST 1

DIRECTIONS: Each question or incomplete statement is followed by several suggested answers or completions. Select the one that BEST answers the question or completes the statement. *PRINT THE LETTER OF THE CORRECT ANSWER IN THE SPACE AT THE RIGHT.*

1. One day an elderly man asks you if he can apply for Social Security at the welfare office.
   Your response should be to
   A. tell him that it is foolish to think he can apply for Social Security at the welfare office
   B. take him back to his apartment because he is too old to be roaming the streets asking questions
   C. explain that Social Security is a federal program and direct him to the nearest Social Security office
   D. call his daughter and tell her that the family should take better care of their father

   1.____

2. One of your duties is to occasionally visit clients. On one occasion, you visit Mrs. B., who needs assistance in referral of her children for day care so that she may enter a job training program. She has postponed completing the referral.
   What should you do in this situation?
   A. Tell her that if she doesn't hurry there will be no room at the day care center and the training program will be closed
   B. Make the arrangements and tell Mrs. B. that she should do what you say
   C. Remember that all people who ask for help are not always ready to receive it and continue to allow Mrs. B. to complete the referral by herself
   D. The next time Mrs. B. asks for help, see that she gets it as slowly as possible

   2.____

3. Assume that you are trying to contact a community group to offer to meet with their representative to explain a new agency policy about intake procedures.
   In order to "get your message across," you should
   A. write a short concise letter explaining why you want to meet with them and when you will be available
   B. write a short letter stating only that it is important that they contact you in order to arrange a meeting
   C. ask a secretary to help you because you do not really like to write to groups
   D. call the agency rather than write since you know someone there

   3.____

4. It is necessary for you to call the director of a head start center in order to discuss   4._____
   a training program for teaching aides. The operator asks who you are and
   what you wish to discuss with the director.
   Your response should be to
   A. tell her that you would rather explain to the director and you want to
      speak to her immediately
   B. identify yourself, your department, and the nature of your business with
      the director
   C. hang up and try to call again when another operator is on duty
   D. tell your supervisor that the operator at the head start center is rude and
      you would rather not be asked to call there again

5. Mr. A. wants her children to go to summer camp. She has receive the request   5._____
   forms, but does not understand all of the questions and you are asked to help
   her complete them. She comes to the office at the appointed time.
   Of the following, the action you should take is to
   A. tell her she has taken so long that maybe the children will not go to camp
   B. see her as quickly as possible, explain the questions to her, and help her
      in completing the forms
   C. help her, but tell her she will have to learn to read better and refer her to
      an evening school
   D. fill out the forms or her by yourself

6. Mrs. B. needs a referral to the cancer clinic. You contact the clinic and make   6._____
   arrangements for her visit. You go to her home to inform her about the time
   because she has no phone. She thanks you for your help and then offers you
   a piece of jewelry that appears to be rather expensive.
   Of the following, the action you should take is to
   A. take the gift because you don't want to hurt her feelings
   B. tell her that she is foolish and should spend her money on herself
   C. explain to her that you are pleased with her thoughtfulness, but you are
      unable to accept the gift
   D. refuse the gift and get someone else to make referrals in the future
      because she is trying to pay you for your help

7. Mrs. C., a seemingly healthy, intelligent woman whose husband is disabled, and   7._____
   who works part-time, asks for help in getting homemaker services.
   Of the following, the action you should take is to
   A. give Mrs. C. the necessary information and help her get the services
   B. tell Mrs. C. that you do not feel she needs these services since her
      husband is capable of helping
   C. make note of her request since you do not feel it is urgent
   D. refer her to a caseworker since she obviously needs help in defining her
      role as a woman

8. When you are interviewing clients, it is important to notice and record how they   8._____
   say what they say—angrily, nervously, or with "body English"—because these
   signs may

A. tell you that the client's words are the opposite of what the client feels and you may need to dig to find out what those feelings are
B. be the prelude to violent behavior which no aide is prepared to handle
C. show that the client does not really deserve serious consideration
D. be important later should you be asked to defend what you did for the client

9. You are recording a visit you have made with a client who was angry and abusive to you during the interview. At one point, you lost your temper and said some things that you immediately regretted. You are embarrassed to record that you lost your temper.
However, it would be desirable to record this MAINLY because
   A. you would feel guilty if you did not record it
   B. your supervisor might hear about it from the client, so it would be better to have it written down from your point of view
   C. your supervisor can use the information to help you to improve your skills
   D. it is agency policy to write down everything

10. Through one of your clients you learn that a day care program's hours have been extended. You confirm this information with the day care center.
It is then MOST important for you to
   A. make a note of this fact, since it will mean you have to change your schedule in working with the client
   B. add this information to your personal resource file so that you can refer other clients to the day dare program
   C. inform your supervisor of the new information so that it can be added to the central resource file
   D. ignore the information, since your client does not need to have her child in day care for any extra hours

11. You are sent to a meeting of day-care parents to explain the programs of your agency. One of the parents becomes very angry, saying that welfare departments treat people like animals.
You should remain as calm as possible and say to the parent that
   A. he is right, but you have no control over what your agency does
   B. he is disrupting the meeting and you have come to explain a program, not to listen to complaints
   C. you understand his feelings and that sometimes clients do not get the services they wish as quickly as possible; however, you will do whatever you can to assist him
   D. he should call your supervisor tomorrow and make an appointment to discuss his feelings

12. Assume that you receive a telephone call from a very angry father. His daughter took money from his wallet, and he wants the caseworker to control the daughter. He yells, screams, and swears at you.
What is the BEST way for you to respond?

A. Hang up because you are not responsible for his daughter's actions. He shouldn't scream and swear at you.
B. Remember to be courteous and polite at all times, never losing your temper
C. Transfer the call to the supervisor because you are concerned about the father's unreasonableness and do not want the responsibility of dealing with him
D. Tell him that behavior such as he is demonstrating is the reason his daughter steals from him

13. Mrs. D.'s son, aged 12, has been getting into difficulty in the neighborhood. At a community meeting, she asks your help in finding worthwhile activities for him. It is APPROPRIATE for you to respond to her because
    A. you should have knowledge of the social services available in the neighborhood and the activities they offer
    B. you have known Mrs. D. and her family for several years and know how much trouble she has had with her son
    C. it is your job to do what the caseworker assigns to you without question
    D. you are concerned about impressing Mrs. D with your knowledge

14. Several clients live in your neighborhood. They know that you work for the human resources administration. One day one of them tells you that there is a rumor that another client is pregnant and asks if this is true. You know from a past discussion with the caseworker that this client is pregnant.
    The BEST answer for you to give would be to
    A. tell her it is none of her business and if she wants to know, she should ask the caseworker
    B. ask her who told her that this client is pregnant
    C. explain that anything told to the agency is held in confidence and will not be shared with anyone else
    D. tell her you don't know, but will ask when you get back to the office and let her know later

15. The area senior citizens group asks for an agency representative to discuss old-age assistance and new SSI regulations. Your supervisor asks you to attend this meeting; however, you do not wish to go because you really do not feel that you work well with older people. In fact, you don't like them very much.
    What should be your response?
    A. Tell the supervisor that you cannot go because you have an appointment with the doctor that day
    B. Get another worker to go for you and assume his task while he is gone
    C. Explain to your supervisor what problems you have in working with old-age clients
    D. Go, because you should do the tasks that are assigned to you according to your job description

16. At a center where you are distributing literature about agency programs, a citizen comes up to you and begins to complain loudly about agency programs. What should be your response?
    A. Call the police and have the complainer removed from the center
    B. Tell him that you do not make policy; suggest that he go to the office and complain
    C. Remain as calm as possible and ask that he discuss the complaints with you calmly. If necessary, make an appointment with him
    D. Yell at him since this seems to be the way he relates to agency people

16.____

17. A community group is having a training program. You are sent to explain agency policy and answer questions.
    Providing this type of contact between the agency and community groups is PROPER because
    A. you like people and are a good public speaker
    B. it is the responsibility of the agency to cooperate with community groups in order to help the public to be well-informed about agency policy
    C. you were once in the same training program and understand the kind of people who are being trained
    D. once in a while everyone should have the opportunity to speak to a community group

17.____

18. While you are assisting in the intake area, a young man who is applying is cooperative but begins to ask you personal questions: your age, where you live, whether you have children, and other similar questions.
    You are disturbed by these questions, so you should
    A. tell him that agency policy does not allow you to answer personal questions and send him to another intake worker
    B. tell him it is your responsibility to ask questions, not his
    C. tell your supervisor that you do not want to work in intake because clients can get too nosy and you get nervous
    D. avoid answering personal questions and try to get him to return to the purpose of the interview

18.____

19. You are assigned to the reception area for the day. A mother arrives in the office with three small children. In a rage, she says that she does not have enough money to feed the children and demands that you find a home for them.
    The BEST action for you to take should be to
    A. call a security officer and have him remove her and the children from the office
    B. attempt to calm her down by listening to her, attend to the children's needs and call for a supervisor
    C. take the children from her and ask her to leave at once
    D. call the supervisor and security because it is their job to take care of abusive clients

19.____

20. Assume that you are interviewing a young unwed mother who has recently arrived in the city from Alabama. She is a likable girl and is very cooperative. However, it is difficult to understand the meaning of her conversation due to her accent and different use of words.
You would like to establish a good relationship with her, so you should FIRST
    A. suggest that she go to evening school so that she can learn to speak like other people in the city
    B. tell her that you don't understand her sometimes and you would appreciate it if she would explain what she means
    C. take another worker with you on visits to help you in the interview
    D. try to find a worker in the agency who has a similar background and have the case handled by the worker

21. A man being interviewed is entitled to Medicaid, but he refuses to sign up for it because he says he cannot accept any form of welfare.
Of the following, the BEST course of action for an aide to take FIRST is to
    A. try to discover the reason for his feeling this way
    B. tell him that he should be glad financial help is available
    C. explain that others cannot get help him if he will not help himself
    D. suggest that he speak to someone who is already on Medicaid

22. Of the following, the outcome of an interview by an aide depends MOS heavily on the
    A. personality of the interviewee
    B. personality of the aide
    C. subject matter of the questions asked
    D. interaction between aide and interviewee

23. Some patients being interviewed are PRIMARILY interested in making a favorable impression. The aide should be aware of the fact that such patients are more likely than other patients to
    A. try to anticipate the answers the interviewer is looking for
    B. answer all questions openly and frankly
    C. try to assume the role of interviewer
    D. be anxious to get the interview over as quickly as possible

24. The type of interview which an aide usually conducts is substantially different from most interviewing situations in all of the following aspects EXCEPT the
    A. setting   B. kinds of clients
    C. techniques employed D. kinds of problems

25. During an interview, an aide uses a "leading question."
This type of question is so-called because it generally
    A. starts a series of questions about one topic
    B. suggests the answer which the aide wants
    C. forms the basis for a following "trick" question
    D. sets, at the beginning, the tone of the interview

KEY (CORRECT ANSWERS)

1.	C	11.	C
2.	C	12.	B
3.	A	13.	A
4.	B	14.	C
5.	B	15.	C
6.	C	16.	C
7.	A	17.	B
8.	A	18.	D
9.	C	19.	B
10.	C	20.	B

21. A
22. D
23. A
24. C
25. B

TEST 2

DIRECTIONS: Each question or incomplete statement is followed by several suggested answers or completions. Select the one that BEST answers the question or completes the statement. *PRINT THE LETTER OF THE CORRECT ANSWER IN THE SPACE AT THE RIGHT.*

1. Miss Lally is an old-age assistance recipient. Her health is not good and it is important that she have three good meals each day. She follows these instructions except on Friday she refuses to eat meat because of her religious beliefs. She will not even substitute fish.
   You are very concerned about this, so you should
   A. tell your supervisor so that she will go to see Miss Lally and make her eat nourishing meals on Friday
   B. call her doctor and tell him so that he will see her and explain to her that fasting is not good for her health
   C. attempt to understand her value system and accept that it is possible that she is acting in good faith with her own values even though they may be harmful to her health
   D. explain to her how important it is that she eat meat each day in order to be in good health and enjoy the remaining years of her life

   1.____

2. Theodore is a junkie. Every cent he can get his hands on legally or illegally is used to supply his habit. You are angry because the junkie is destroying himself and his family. You feel that the courts should punish him for his illegal acts.
   Of the following, the BEST action for you to take is to
   A. suggest to your supervisor that the income maintenance center reduce the family grant, taking out his portion
   B. help his wife to find another apartment for her and the children away from him
   C. call the local police to find out why they are doing nothing about this man's activities in the community
   D. reconsider your ideas about punishment, remembering that punishment alone will not help the man to change his behavior

   2.____

3. You are regularly assigned to taking Sarah Jones and her young son to the clinic. She is a very warm, friendly woman and your relationship with her is good. However, she invited you to come for dinner on Sunday and to go to a school play with her. You would like to accept the invitations because you need weekend activities and you like her.
   What should be your PRIMARY consideration in coming to a decision?
   A. You need friends just as she does, so you should accept the invitations
   B. You are a worker and should not be seen with a client in public places
   C. Decide whether accepting the invitations will help to meet agency needs or will hamper the relationship you are expected to establish
   D. Tell her "no" because it is not a good policy to be on such friendly terms with clients

   3.____

4. Martha's husband has been arrested in a drug raid and she is extremely anxious. Your supervisor asks that you visit her to determine ways in which the agency may help her. You visit and find her weeping; the house and the children have obviously been neglected.
The BEST thing for you to do is to
   A. tell her to stop crying and help her to clean the apartment and the children
   B. remind her that her husband has been warned and now has to pay for not listening
   C. listen to her, allowing her to express her feelings of fear, loss, and grief, and reassure her of your concern
   D. listen to her but caution her that she is neglecting the home and children because of her anxiety and you may have to ask your supervisor to remove the children if she doesn't get any better

5. Mrs. Dwight's landlord is very slow in making repairs in her apartment. Each time you see her, she complains about this over and over again, calling her landlord names and threatening to report him to the city. She complains to any agency person she meets.
Realizing that these complaints are not getting any action, you should
   A. avoid meeting with her because she is annoying
   B. suggest that she see a doctor because she is irrational and should get some help
   C. ask her what she would like to do about the problem and assist her in carrying out her plans
   D. ask the supervisor to see her because you do not have the skills to help her

6. In the day-to-day operations of the human resources administration, which of the following would you consider to be the PRIMARY function of the agency?
   A. Getting work done to meet city and federal deadlines
   B. Being sure that all of the clients who come to the agency are seen before closing time
   C. Delivering services to those persons who are eligible for assistance
   D. Making sure everyone gets his check on time

7. During the course of an interview you find it is necessary to arrange a special appointment for the client to return for a further interview. After checking your calendar, you tell the client the date she is to come back. The client, however, says she cannot see you on that date because she is to attend a rally at a community center in her neighborhood.
Of the following, your BEST action should be to
   A. let her know that any other day is an inconvenience to you and remind her that the appointment is for her benefit
   B. forget about the special appointment and try to get along with the information you have
   C. explain to her the need for the appointment and ask when she can meet with you
   D. tell her that since the community center is not city-operated, she must keep her appointment with you

8. In working with community groups, it is important that you be able to define what a community is.
Of the following definitions, which is the MOST appropriate?
A community
   A. consists of a group of people living fairly close together in a more or less compact territory, who come together in their chief concerns
   B. is a particular section of a city designated on a census tract
   C. is that portion of a city which constitutes an election district
   D. is a section of a city or town in which a particular ethnic group conducts its social, business, and religious life

8._____

9. The agency has implemented a new policy regarding the intake procedure. You wish to explain and discuss this policy with as many community groups as possible. You make an initial contact by mail.
In order to get your message across well, your letter should be
   A. short and as concise as possible explaining why you want to meet with them, and offer several possible times that you will be available
   B. short, explaining only that it is important that the groups contact you in order to arrange a meeting
   C. drafted by the center's secretary and sent to the usual groups
   D. put in the usual announcement form in the center's newsletter

9._____

10. A group of young welfare mothers want to form an organization that will provide babysitting services for mothers of children who are too young to enroll in a day care center.
What should be your answer to them?
   A. Tell them to try to get the center to change its policy to include young children
   B. Arrange the time to meet with them to offer as much advice and support as possible, since most communities do need this service
   C. Suggest that it may be better that they spend their time taking care of their own children
   D. Ask a social worker to survey the community to determine if such a service is really needed at this time

10._____

11. New regulations have removed the disabled, blind, and old-age assistance cases from the public assistance caseload. Assistance in these categories is given directly by the federal government. A former client has not received his check. The chairman of the senior citizens committee calls and angrily demands that your agency do something in this man's behalf.
In response, you should
   A. answer politely, explaining that your agency is not concerned about OAA clients
   B. arrange to meet with him in order to discuss the new policy
   C. refer him to the Social Security office covering the area where the client lives
   D. ask that he call again when he is calmer so that you may discuss this matter with him

11._____

12. A high school student from the community comes to see you about a homework assignment to write a report on your center.
    The BEST way to help him is to
    A. refer him to a social worker who has daily contact with clients in their homes
    B. contact the boy's teacher and find out why you were not warned of his coming
    C. explain your center's program and answer as many of his questions as you can
    D. give him literature about the welfare system in the city and state

13. Assume that the women's group of the Community Baptist Church has invited you to a Sunday afternoon service to celebrate the tenth anniversary of the pastor. The agency's relationship with the women is good in that they often offer their homes as emergency homes for adult clients.
    What should you do about the invitation?
    A. Do not attend but send them a note congratulating the pastor and explaining that agency personnel do not work on Sundays
    B. Ask a social worker who lives close to the church to go
    C. Accept the invitation if at all possible, attend the service and whatever social hour they may have afterwards
    D. Ignore the invitation since this function has little relationship to your job

14. Suppose that a person you are interviewing becomes angry at some of the questions you have asked, calls you meddlesome and nosy, and states that she will not answer those questions.
    Of the following, which is the BEST action for you to take
    A. Explain the reasons the questions are asked and the importance of the answers
    B. Inform the interviewee that you are only doing your job and advise her that she should answer your questions or leave your office
    C. Report to your supervisor what the interviewee called you and refuse to continue the interview
    D. End the interview and tell the interviewee she will not be serviced by your department

15. Suppose that during the course of an interview the interviewee demands in a very rude way that she be permitted to talk to your supervisor or someone in charge.
    Which of the following is probably the BEST way to handle this situation?
    A. Inform your supervisor of the demand and ask her to speak to the interviewee
    B. Pay no attention to the demands of the interviewee and continue the interview
    C. Report to your supervisor and tell her to get another interviewer for this interviewee
    D. Tell her you are the one "in charge" and that she should talk to you

16. Suppose that a worker asks a client to answer several required but rather personal questions about the family's health history. The client delays and seems embarrassed about giving the answers.
    Of the following, the MOST reasonable response to the client is one which
    A. shows an awareness of the client's efforts to hide something
    B. demonstrates the worker's qualifications for asking such questions
    C. allows this client to be excused from answering the questions
    D. convinces the client that his uneasiness in the situation is understood

17. A representative from a planned parenthood group comes to see you to get information for a community education program.
    You should
    A. check out this group to make sure it is not promoting zero population growth for minority groups
    B. develop a good relationship with him so as to provide better service to clients
    C. make sure they will not encourage unnecessary abortions
    D. refuse to see him

18. A member of a clerical training program is continually late to classes. He explains to you that he has a hard time getting up and asks that you report him on time because he needs to train for a job.
    What should your response be?
    A. Tell him that you get there on time and so should he
    B. Tell him that you do not lie for anyone
    C. Explain that it is your duty to keep accurate records and refer him to a counselor
    D. Tell him that you will cooperate with him but he has to try to do better

19. In a community meeting to explain a new agency policy, you find that the audience has no questions about the policy or your explanations.
    What would be the MOST appropriate response to the silence?
    A. Leave right away before they think of questions
    B. Thank the audience for their attention and assure them that you will be available if there are any questions later
    C. Ask several members in the audience if they understand the new policy
    D. Explain that the audience could not possibly understand all of the policy and they must have questions

20. Assume that you are confronted by an angry member of the public who has not been able to obtain the information he needs from your office. You do not know the answer to his question.
    The BEST thing for you to do would be to
    A. tell him to come back another time, after you have looked up the information
    B. check with your supervisor to find the correct answer

C. tell him to ask in another office, so that you will not lose time looking for the information
D. make up and answer to keep the man satisfied until the right answer is found

---

KEY (CORRECT ANSWERS)

1.	C	11.	C
2.	D	12.	C
3.	C	13.	C
4.	C	14.	A
5.	C	15.	A
6.	C	16.	D
7.	C	17.	B
8.	A	18.	C
9.	A	19.	B
10.	B	20.	B

EXAMINATION SECTION

TEST 1

DIRECTIONS: Each question or incomplete statement is followed by several suggested answers or completions. Select the one that BEST answers the question or completes the statement. *PRINT THE LETTER OF THE CORRECT ANSWER IN THE SPACE AT THE RIGHT.*

1. A client tells you that he is extremely upset by the treatment that he received from Center personnel at the information desk.
 Which of the following is the BEST way to handle this complaint during the interview?
    A. Explain to the client that he probably misinterpreted what occurred at the information desk
    B. Let the client express his feelings and then proceed with the interview
    C. Tell the client that you are not concerned with the personnel at the information desk
    D. Escort the client to the information desk to find out what really happened

1.____

2. As a worker in the foster home division, you are reviewing a case record to determine whether a 13-year-old boy, in foster care because of neglect and mistreatment by his natural parents, should be returned home. The natural parents, who want to take the child back, have been in family counseling, with encouraging result, and have improved their living conditions.
 Of the following, it would be appropriate to recommend that the child
    A. remain with the foster parents, since this is a documented case of child abuse
    B. remain with the foster parents until they are ready to send him home
    C. be returned to his natural parents, since they have made positive efforts to change their behavior toward the child
    D. be returned to his natural parents, because continued separation will cause irreparable damage to the child

2.____

3. You are finishing an interview with a client in which you have explained to her the procedure she must go through to apply for income maintenance.
 Of the following, the BEST way for you to make sure that she has fully understood the procedure is too ask her
    A. whether she feels she has understood your explanation of the procedure
    B. whether she has any questions to ask you about the procedure
    C. to describe the procedure to you in her own words
    D. a few questions to test her understanding of the procedure

3.____

4. Mrs. Carey, a widow with five children, has come to the field office to seek foster care for her 13-year-old daughter, who has often been truant from school and has recently been caught shoplifting. Mrs. Carey says that she cannot maintain a proper home environment for the other four children and deal with her daughter at the same time.

4.____

Of the following, you should FIRST
- A. process Mrs. Carey's request for placement of her daughter in a foster care agency
- B. interview both Mrs. Carey and her daughter to get a more complete picture of the situation
- C. suggest to Mrs. Care that she might be able to manage if she obtained homemaker services
- D. warn the daughter that she will be sent away from home if she does not change her behavior

5. During a group orientation meeting with couples who wish to adopt babies through your agency, one couple asks you how they should deal with the question of whether the child should be told that he is adopted.
Of the following, your BEST response to this couple is to
- A. tell them to conceal from the child the fact that he is adopted
- B. suggest that they lead the child to believe that his natural parents are dead
- C. tell them to inform the child that they know nothing about his natural parents
- D. explore with them their feelings about revealing to the child that he is adopted

6. You are beginning an investigation of an anonymous complaint that a welfare client has a concealed bank account.
Of the following, the FIRST step you should generally take in conducting this investigation is to
- A. confront the client with the complaint during an office interview
- B. try to track down the source of the anonymous complaint
- C. make a surprise visit to the client in his home to question him
- D. gather any available information from bank and agency records

7. When investigating the location of an absent parent, the worker frequently interviews the parent's friends and neighbors. The worker often writes down the information given by the person interviewed and, at the end of the interview, summarizes the information to the person.
For the worker to do this is, generally,
- A. *good practice*, because the person interviewed will be impressed by the efficiency of the worker
- B. *poor practice*, because the person interviewed may become impatient with the worker for repeating the information
- C. *good practice*, because the person interviewed has an opportunity to correct any errors the worker may have in recording the information
- D. *poor practice*, because summarizing the information may encourage the person to waste time adding and changing information

8. During an interview for the purpose of investigating a charge of child abuse, a client first denied that she had abused her child, but then burst into tears and promised that she *will never do it again.*
Of the following, the MOST appropriate action for the worker to take in this situation is to
   A. tell the client that, since she has already lied, it is difficult to believe that she will keep her promise
   B. show a concern for the client's feelings but tell her that you will have to report your findings and refer her for help
   C. determine the extent to which the child was abused and close the case if no permanent harm was done
   D. explain to the client that she has already done enough harm to the child and you must, therefore, recommend placement

8.____

9. As a worker involved in locating absent parents, you have obtained information indicating that the address for the putative father is the same as the client's address.
In order to determine whether, in fact, the client and putative father are living together, of the following, it would be MOST appropriate to
   A. visit the address and question the neighbors and superintendent about the putative father
   B. visit the client to ask her why she has concealed the fact that the putative father is living with her
   C. file the information in the case folder and wait for confirming information
   D. close the client's case and issue a recoupment notice to the putative father

9.____

10. A client claims that she never received a welfare check that was due her. As part of your investigation of her claim, you obtain from the bank a copy of the check, which has been endorsed with her name and cashed.
Of the following, the BEST procedure for you to follow in this investigation is to
   A. end the investigation immediately, since the client's claim cannot be proved
   B. interview the client and show her the copy of the cashed check
   C. tell the client that you have evidence that her claim is false
   D. say nothing about the cashed check and try to trap the client in a false statement

10.____

11. As part of the investigation to locate an absent father, you make a field visit to interview one of the father's friends. Before beginning the interview, you identify yourself to the friend and show him your official identification.
For you to do this is, generally,
   A. *good practice,* because the friend will have proof that you are authorized to make such confidential investigations
   B. *poor practice,* because the friend may not answer your questions when he knows why you are interviewing him

11.____

C. *good practice*, because your supervisor can confirm from the friend that you actually made the interview
D. *poor practice*, because the friend may warn the absent father that your agency is looking for him

12. As a field office worker you are investigating a citizen's complaint charging a mother of three children with child neglect. The mother tells you that her husband has become depressed after losing his job and is often abusive to her, and that this situation has made her feel anxious and has made it difficult for her to care for the children properly.
Which one of the following is the BEST way for you to respond to this situation?
    A. Tell the mother that she must do everything possible to help her husband find a job
    B. Arrange to meet the husband so you can explain to him the consequences of his behavior
    C. Investigate the complaint, report your findings, and refer the family for counseling or other appropriate services
    D. Suggest that the family obtain homemaker services so that the mother can go to work

12._____

13. You are interviewing a client in his home as part of your investigation of an anonymous complaint that he has been receiving Medicaid fraudulently. During the interview, the client frequently interrupts your questions to discuss the hardships of his life and the bitterness he feels about his medical condition.
Of the following, the BEST way for you to deal with these discussions is to
    A. cut them off abruptly, since the client is probably just trying to avoid answering your questions
    B. listen patiently, since these discussions may be helpful to the client and may give you information for your investigation
    C. remind the client that you are investigating a complaint against him and he must answer directly
    D. seek to gain the client's confidence by discussing any personal or medical problems which you yourself may have

13._____

14. While interviewing an absent father to determine his ability to pay child support, you realize that his answers to some of your questions contradict his answers to other questions.
Of the following, the BEST way for you to try to get accurate information from the father is to
    A. confront him with his contradictory answers and demand an explanation from him
    B. use your best judgment as to which of his answers are accurate and question him accordingly
    C. tell him that he has misunderstood your questions and that he must clarify his answers
    D. ask him the same questions in different words and follow up his answers with related questions

14._____

15. You are assigned to investigate a complaint of child neglect made against a minority mother by her non-minority neighbor. During an interview with you, the neighbor states that the mother allows her children to run around the streets half-dressed till late at night, and adds: *Of course, what can you expect from any of those people anyway?*
Your MOST appropriate action is to
    A. end the investigation, since the neighbor is clearly too prejudiced to be reliable
    B. tell the mother that the neighbor has made a complaint of child neglect against her
    C. seek evidence to support the complaint of child neglect made by the neighbor
    D. continue the interview with the neighbor in an attempt to get at the root of his prejudice against the mother

16. You are interviewing a couple with regard to available services for the husband's aged mother. During the interview, the husband casually mentions that he and his wife are thinking about becoming foster parents and would like to get some information on foster care programs offered through the Department of Social Services.
Of the following agencies within social services, the MOST appropriate one for you to refer this couple to is
    A. family and adult services
    B. special services for children
    C. bureau of child support
    D. special services for adults

17. You have been helping one of your clients to obtain medical assistance for her two young children. Accidentally, you obtain evidence that the client may be involved in a criminal scheme to collect duplicate welfare checks at several different addresses.
Of the following offices of the Department of Social Services, the MOST appropriate one to which you should report this evidence is
    A. the inspector general
    B. case intake and management
    C. the general counsel
    D. income support

Questions 18-25.

DIRECTIONS: Questions 18 through 25 are to be answered SOLELY on the basis of the Fact Situation and Report Form.

FACT SITUATION

On June 5, 2020, Mary Adams (Case No. 2095732), living at 1507 Montague Street, Apt. 3C, Brooklyn, New York, applied and was accepted for public assistance for herself and her three dependent children. Her husband, John, had left their home after an argument the previous week and had not returned, leaving Mrs. Adams without funds of any kind. She had tried to contact him at his place of employment, but was told that he had resigned several days prior to her call. When the case worker questioned Mrs. Adams about her husband's employment, income, and bank accounts, Mrs. Adams stated that he had done carpentry work during most of the years he had worked; his last known employer had been the Avco Lumber Company, 309 Amber Street, Queens, New York, where he had earned a weekly salary of $300. She then showed the case worker two bankbooks in her husband's name, which indicated a balance of $500 in one account and $275 in the other. A visit to Mr. Brown, a neighbor of the Adams', by the case worker, revealed that Mr. Adams had also told Mr. Brown about the existence of the bankbooks. A visit to the Avco Lumber Company by the case worker confirmed that Mr. Adams' gross salary had been $300 a week. This visit also revealed that Mr. Adams was a member of the Woodworkers' Union, Local #3, and that Mr. Adams' previous home address for the period February '09 to June '15 was 1109 Wellington Street, Brooklyn, New York.

REPORT FORM

A. **CLIENT:**
   1. Name:_____
   2. Address:_____
   3. Case No:_____
   4. Acceptance Date:_____
   5. No. of Dependent Children:_____

B. **ABSENT PARENT:**
   1. Name:_____
   2. Date of Birth:_____
   3. Place of Birth:_____
   4. Present Address:_____
   5. Regular Occupation:_____
   6. Union Affiliation:_____
   7. Name of Last Employer:_____
   8. Address of Last Employer:_____
   9. a. Weekly Earnings (Gross):_____
      b. How Verified:_____
   10. a. Weekly Earnings (Net):_____
       b. How Verified:_____
   11. a. Amount of Bank Accounts:_____
       b. How Verified:_____
   12. Social Security No.:_____
   13. Last Known Home Address:_____
   14. Previous Address:_____

---

18. Based on the information given in the Fact Situation, the MOST appropriate of the following entries for Item B.11.b is:
    A. Revealed to case worker by Mrs. Adams
    B. Confirmed by visit to Mr. Brown
    C. Revealed by Woodworkers' Union, Local #7
    D. Confirmed by bankbooks shown by Mrs. Adams

7 (#1)

19. The one of the following which BEST answers Item B.4 is 19.____
    A. Unknown
    B. c/o Avco Lumber Company
    C. 1109 Wellington Street, Brooklyn, New York
    D. 1507 Montague Street, Brooklyn, New York

20. Based on the information given in the Fact Situation, it is NOT possible to 20.____
    answer Item
    A. A.2   B. A.5   C. B.6   D. B.10

21. The one of the following which would be LEAST helpful in tracing the missing 21.____
    parent is information found in Item
    A. B.12   B. B.10.a   C. B.6   D. B.1

22. Based on the information given in the Fact Situation, it is MOST likely that 22.____
    the same entry would be made for Items
    A. A.1 and B.1   B. A.4 and B.2
    C. B.9.a and B.10.a   D. A.2 and B.13

23. Based on the information in the Fact Situation, the entry: 1109 Wellington 23.____
    Street, Brooklyn, New York would MOST likely be placed for Item
    A. A.2   B. B.4   C. B.8   D. B.14

24. The one of the following items that can be answered based on the information 24.____
    given in the Fact Situation is
    A. B.2   B. B.3   C. B.9.b   D. B.12

25. Based on the information given in the Fact Situation, the figure 775 would 25.____
    appear in the entry for
    A. A.3   B. B.12   C. B.9.a   D. B.11.a

KEY (CORRECT ANSWERS)

1. B
2. C
3. C
4. B
5. D

6. D
7. C
8. B
9. A
10. B

11. A
12. C
13. B
14. D
15. C

16. B
17. A
18. D
19. A
20. D

21. B
22. D
23. D
24. C
25. D

TEST 2

DIRECTIONS: Each question or incomplete statement is followed by several suggested answers or completions. Select the one that BEST answers the question or completes the statement. *PRINT THE LETTER OF THE CORRECT ANSWER IN THE SPACE AT THE RIGHT.*

1. A worker in a senior adult center is approached by one of his clients, an elderly man living alone and suffering from severe arthritis, who asks him how to go about obtaining homemaker services through the Department of Social Services.
   Of the following, the MOST appropriate office of the department to which the worker should refer this client is
   A. income support
   B. protective services for adults
   C. income maintenance
   D. case intake and management

   1.____

2. Workers assigned to locate absent parents frequently ask various governmental agencies to search their records for information useful in determining the address of the person they are seeking.
   Of the following, which is likely to be useful MOST frequently for this purpose is the
   A. motor vehicle bureau
   B. office of the district attorney
   C. department of investigation
   D. health and hospitals corporation

   2.____

Questions 3-7.

DIRECTIONS: Questions 3 through 7 are to be answered SOLELY on the basis of the following Fact Situation and Preliminary Investigation Form.

FACT SITUATION

COMPLAINT:
On March 1, Mrs. Mona Willard, a neighbor of the Smith family, reported to the Police Department that the Smith children were being severely neglected, and she requested that an investigation be conducted. She based her complaint on the fact that, since the time three weeks ago when Janet Smith's husband, Charles, deserted Mrs. Smith and their two children, John, age 2, and Darlene, age 4, the children have been seen wandering in the neighborhood at all hours, inadequately dressed against the cold.

INVESTIGATION:
Investigation by the Police Department and the Department of Social Services revealed that the above charge was true and, further, that Mrs. Smith had inflicted cruel and harsh physical treatment upon the children in an attempt to discipline them. The children were immediately removed from their parent's care and placed in a medical facility for tests and observation. It was found that the children were suffering from serious malnutrition and anemia and that they also showed signs of emotional disturbance.

2 (#2)

CASE ACTION DECISION:
Conferences which you, the case worker, have held with Dr. Charles Jordan, a physician treating Mrs. Smith, and with Ellen Farraday, a psychiatric social worker from the Mental Health Consultation Center, confirm that Mrs. Smith is emotionally unstable at the present time and cannot care for her children. A written report from the Chief Resident Physician at the hospital where the children have been placed indicates that both children are presently doing well, but when released will need the security of an emotionally stable atmosphere. It has therefore been decided that placement in a foster home is necessary for the children until such time as Mrs. Smith is judged to be capable of caring for them.

PRELIMINARY INVESTIGATION FORM

1. Child(ren) in Need of Protection:
    a. Name(s):_____
    b. Age(s):_____
2. Alleged Perpetrator:
    a. Name_____
    b. Relationship_____
3. Present Status of Child(ren):
    ☐ a. Remaining with Subject Pending Investigation
    ☐ b. Removed to Relatives
    ☐ c. Removed to Foster Care
    ☐ d. In Hospital
    ☐ e. Other
4. Actions or Services Needed for Child(ren)
    ☐ a. Housekeeper
    ☐ b. Homemaker
    ☐ c. Day Care
    ☐ d. Home Attendant
    ☐ e. Relatives
    ☐ f. Foster Care
5. Contacts Made to Support Case Action Decision

	I Phone	II Personal	III Written
a. Medical; School	☐	☐	☐
b. Relatives	☐	☐	☐
c. Social Agency	☐	☐	☐
d. Other	☐	☐	☐

3. The one of the following that should be entered in space 2.b is 3.____
    A. mother   B. father   C. neighbor   D. physician

4. The one of the following boxes that should be checked in Item 3 is 4.____
    A. a   B. c   C. d   D. e

5. The one of the following boxes that should be checked in Item 4 is 5.____
    A. a   B. c   C. d   D. f

6. Based on the information given in the Fact Situation, the boxes that should be checked off in Item 5 are:
   A. a-II, a-III, C-II
   B. a-II, c-II, c-III
   C. a-I, a-II, a-III
   D. b-II, c-I, c-II

6.____

7. The one of the following that would CORRECTLY appear as part of the entry

Questions 8-12.

DIRECTIONS: Questions 8 through 12 are to be answered SOLELY on the basis of the information contained in the following passage.

It is desirable, whenever possible, to have long-term elderly patients return to their own homes after hospitalization, provided that the medical condition is not acute. Of course, there must be room for the patient; the family must be able to provide some necessary care; and a physician's services must be available. Although the patient's family may be able to provide most services for the patient in his own home, this is generally unlikely because of the nature of the illness and the patient's need for a variety of services. Recently, hospital personnel, public health workers, visiting nurse associations, and community leaders have been developing home-care programs, which make the services of the hospital available to the patient who is not ill enough to require the concentrated technical facilities of a general hospital, but who is unable to attend an outpatient clinic or a physician's office. These services are those of the physician, visiting nurse, physical therapist, occupational therapist, social worker, and homemaker, as needed. There is also provision for readmission to the hospital for specific purposes and return to home care.

8. According to the above passage, it would be UNDESIRABLE to have an elderly patient return to his own home after hospitalization when the patient
   A. requires the services of doctor
   B. may be in immediate danger due to his medical condition
   C. is under physical or occupational therapy
   D. cannot go to the outpatient clinic of the hospital

8.____

9. According to the above passage, the *services of the hospital* which are made available by home-care programs include those of
   A. dietitians
   B. visiting nurses
   C. public health administers
   D. community workers

9.____

10. The one of the following statements about home-care programs which is BEST supported by the above paragraph is that home-care programs
    A. have been developed in part by hospital personnel
    B. relieve workloads of hospital personnel
    C. decrease public expenditures for hospitalization of the elderly
    D. reduce readmissions of elderly patients to hospitals

10.____

11. According to the above passage, home-care programs would be LEAST likely to include the services of a
    A. homemaker
    B. social worker
    C. physician
    D. hospital technician

11.____

12. It may be inferred from the above passage that a MAJOR purpose of home-care programs is to
    A. increase the demand for physicians, nurses, and other medical personnel
    B. provide patients in their homes with services similar to those provided in hospitals
    C. reduce the need for general hospitals and outpatient clinics
    D. relieve the family of their responsibility of caring for the patient

12.____

Questions 13-17.

DIRECTIONS: Questions 13 through 17 are to be answered SOLELY on the basis of the information contained in the following Duties Statement.

DUTIES STATEMENT OF THE VIOLATION CENTER (VC) CASE WORKER

1. Receives telephone, mail, and in-person reports of suspected violations from mandated and non-mandated sources, as well as from the New York State Violation Bureau (NYSVB), on form DSS-555, within 48 hours, to the Central Office of VC, 265 Church Street, New York, N.Y.

2. Completes in-office portion of DSS-555 received from mandated sources as fully as possible. Checks that report summary is specific, factual, and detailed. (See NYSVB instructions on Page 213)

3. When DSS-555 is received, clears Central Office of VC for any previous record of violation on file in Central Office. If record exists, enters additional information from file record on to DSS-555. Also requests Central Office Clerk to provide appropriate record number of previous record and enters additional information from file record on to DSS-555. Also requests Central Office Clerk to provide appropriate record number of previous record and enters it in correct box on form.

4. Determines appropriate Central Office Sex Code and Reporting Source Code for each violation. (The Codes are in the VC Manual.) The codes are then entered on the bottom of the reverse side of the DSS-555.

5. Determines appropriate Service Area Code for the address in the summary. The address is the location of the violation, if known. (If the location of the violation is unknown, the address of the primary witness shall be used.) Enters Service Area Code on reverse of DSS-555. All report summaries involving violations by N.Y.C. employees are sent to the Manhattan Borough Office of VC for clearance and transmittal to BEM.

---

13. According to the above Duties Statement, when a report of a suspected violation is received, a written summary of their report on DSS-555 must be sent within 48 hours by
    A. mandated sources
    B. non-mandated sources
    C. the NYSVB
    D. mandated and non-mandated sources, as well as by the NYSVB

13.____

14. From the above Duties Statement, it may be *inferred* that the case worker whose duties are described is MOST likely assigned to
    A. the Manhattan Borough Office of VC
    B. the New York State Violation Bureau
    C. the Central Office of VC
    D. BEM

15. According to the above Duties Statement, the Central Office Sex Code is entered on the DSS-555
    A. on the opposite side from the Service Area Code
    B. on the front of the form
    C. above the Service Area Code on the form
    D. on the bottom of the back of the form

16. According to the above Duties Statement, a case worker can determine the appropriate Reporting Source Code for a violation by consulting
    A. NYSVB Instructions
    B. the Central Office Clerk
    C. the VC Manual
    D. the Service Area Code

17. As used in paragraph 2 of the above Duties Statement, the word *detailed* means MOST NEARLY
    A. full descriptive
    B. complicated
    C. of considerable length
    D. well-written

Questions 18-25.

DIRECTIONS: Questions 18 through 25 are to be answered SOLELY on the basis of the following Semi-Monthly Family Allowance Schedule for Maintenance of Legally Responsible Relative (Figure No. 1) and Conversion Table (Figure 2) given on the following pages and the information and case situations given below).

FIGURE NO. 1

SEMI-MONTHLY FAMILY ALLOWANCE SCHEDULE FOR MAINTENANCE OF LEGALLY RESPONSIBLE RELATIVE AND DEPENDENTS BASED UPON TOTAL NUMBER OF PERSONS IN PRESENT HOUSEHOLD. (ALL SURPLUS IS TO BE USED AS CONTRIBUTION TO RECIPIENTS OF PUBLIC ASSISTANCE.)

TOTAL NUMBER OF PERSONS IN PRESENT HOUSEHOLD	ONE	TWO	THREE	FOUR	FIVE	SIX	EACH ADDITIONAL PERSON
SEMI-MONTHLY FAMILY ALLOWANCE	$1,600	$1,915	$2,200	$2,605	$2,800	$3,205	$350

FIGURE NO. 2
CONVERSION TABLE – WEEKLY TO SEMI-MONTHLY AMOUNTS

DOLLARS				CENTS			
Weekly Amount	Semi-Monthly Amount	Weekly Amount	Semi-Monthly Amount	Weekly Amount	Semi-Monthly Amount	Weekly Amount	Semi-Monthly Amount
$10	$21.70	$510.00	$1105.00	$0.10	$0.20	$5.10	$11.10
20.00	86.70	520.00	1126.70	0.20	0.40	5.20	11.30
30.00	65.00	530.00	1148.30	0.30	0.70	5.30	11.50
40.00	86.70	540.00	1170.00	0.40	0.90	5.40	11.70
50.00	108.30	550.00	1191.70	0.50	1.10	5.50	11.90
60.00	130.00	560.00	1213.30	0.60	1.30	5.60	12.10
70.00	151.70	570.00	1235.00	0.70	1.50	5.70	12.40
80.00	173.30	580.00	1256.70	1.00	1.70	5.80	12.60
90.00	195.00	590.00	1278.30	0.90	2.00	5.90	12.80
100.00	216.70	600.00	1300.00	1.00	2.20	6.00	13.00
110.00	238.30	610.00	1321.70	1.10	2.40	6.10	13.20
120.00	260.00	620.00	1343.30	1.20	2.60	6.20	13.40
130.00	281.70	630.00	1365.00	1.30	2.80	6.30	13.70
140.00	303.30	640.00	1386.70	1.40	3.00	6.40	13.90
150.00	325.00	650.00	1408.30	1.50	3.30	6.50	14.10
160.00	346.70	660.00	1430.00	1.60	3.50	6.60	14.30
170.00	368.30	670.00	1451.40	1.70	3.70	6.70	14.50
180.00	390.00	680.00	1473.30	1.80	3.90	6.80	14.70
190.00	411.70	690.00	1495.00	1.90	4.10	6.90	15.00
200.00	433.30	700.00	1516.70	2.00	4.30	7.00	15.20
210.00	455.00	710.00	1538.30	2.10	4.60	7.10	15.40
220.00	476.70	720.00	1560.00	2.20	4.80	7.20	15.60
230.00	498.30	730.00	1581.70	2.30	5.00	7.30	15.80
240.00	520.00	740.00	1603.30	2.40	5.20	7.40	16.00
250.00	541.70	750.00	1625.00	2.50	5.40	7.50	16.30
260.00	563.30	760.00	1646.70	2.60	5.60	7.60	16.50
270.00	585.00	770.00	1668.30	2.70	5.90	7.70	16.70
280.00	606.70	780.00	690.00	2.80	6.10	7.80	16.90
290.00	628.30	790.00	1711.70	2.90	6.30	7.90	17.10
300.00	650.00	800.00	1733.30	3.00	6.50	8.00	17.30
310.00	671.70	810.00	1755.00	3.10	6.70	8.10	17.60
320.00	693.30	820.00	1776.70	3.20	6.90	8.20	17.80
330.00	715.00	830.00	1798.30	3.30	7.20	8.30	18.00
340.00	736.70	840.00	1820.00	3.40	7.40	8.40	18.20
350.00	783.00	850.00	1841.70	3.50	7.60	8.50	18.40
360.00	780.00	860.00	1863.30	3.60	7.80	8.60	18.60
370.00	801.70	870.00	1885.00	3.70	8.00	8.70	18.90
380.00	823.30	880.00	1906.70	3.80	8.20	8.80	19.10
390.00	845.00	890.00	1928.30	3.90	8.50	8.90	19.30
400.00	866.70	900.00	1950.00	4.00	8.70	9.00	19.50
410.00	888.30	910.00	1971.70	4.10	8.90	9.10	19.70
420.00	910.00	920.00	1993.30	4.20	9.10	9.20	19.90
430.00	931.70	930.00	2015.00	4.30	9.30	9.30	20.20
440.00	953.30	940.00	2036.70	40.40	9.50	9.40	20.40
450.00	975.00	950.00	2058.30	40.50	9.80	9.50	20.60
460.00	996.70	960.00	2080.00	4.60	10.00	9.60	20.80
470.00	1018.30	970.00	2101.70	4.70	10.20	9.70	21.00
480.00	1040.00	980.00	2123.30	4.80	10.40	9.80	21.20
490.00	1061.70	990.00	2145.00	4.90	10.60	9.90	21.50
500.00	1083.30	1000.00	2166.70	5.00	10.80		

7 (#2)

INFORMATION

Legally responsible relatives living apart from persons on public assistance are asked to contribute toward the support of these persons. The amount of contribution depends on several factors, such as the number of persons in the legally responsible relative's present household who are dependent on his income (including himself), the amount of his gross income, and his expenses incident to employment. Since his contribution is computed on a semi-monthly basis, all figures must be broken down into semi-monthly amounts. Weekly amounts can be converted into semi-monthly amounts by using the conversion table on page 6.

The amount of supported is computed as follows:

1. Determine total weekly gross income (the wages or salary before payroll deductions) of legally responsible relative.
2. Deduct all weekly expenses incident to employment such as federal, state, and city income taxes, Social Security payments, State Disability Insurance payments, union dues, cost of transportation, and $10.00 maximum per work day for lunch.
3. Remaining income shall be considered as weekly net income of legally responsible relative.
4. Convert weekly net income to semi-monthly net income, using data in Figure No. 2.
5. Semi-monthly net income is compared to the semi-monthly allowance (see Figure No. 1). If there is an excess of net income, then that amount is considered available as the contribution to the public assistance household. If the semi-monthly allowance is greater than the semi-monthly net income, then there is an income deficit, and there is no income available as a contribution to the public assistance household.
6. The formula for computing the semi-monthly contribution is:
Semi-Monthly Net Income • Semi-Monthly Family Allowance = Semi-Monthly Amount of Income Available Towards Contribution to Public Assistance Household

Case Situation No. 1:

Mr. Andrew Young is separated from his wife and family and lives with one dependent in a 3-room furnished apartment. Mr. Young is employed as a dishwasher and his gross wages are $1,000 per week. He is employed 5 days a week and spends $14.40 a day for carfare. He spends $20.00 a work day on lunch. His weekly salary deductions are as follows:

Federal Income Tax	$142.30
State Income Tax	26.00
City Income Tax	9.80
Social Security	62.10
New York State Disability Insurance	5.30
Union Due	5.00

Mr. Young's wife and two children, for whom he is legally responsible, are currently receiving public assistance.

8 (#2)

18. The weekly amount that Mr. Young contributes toward Social Security, New York State Disability Insurance, Income Taxes, and Union Dues is MOST NEARLY
    A. $214.70   B. $250.50   C. $320.50   D. $370.50

18.____

19. The total amount of all weekly expenses incident to Mr. Young's employment which should be deducted from his weekly gross earnings is MOST NEARLY
    A. $214.70   B. $250.50   C. $370.50   D. $420.50

19.____

20. Which one of the following amounts is Mr. Young's semi-monthly net income?
    A. $1259.00   B. $1363.90   C. $1623.90   D. $1701.50

20.____

21. The semi-monthly amount of income available to the contribution to Mr. Young's wife and two children is MOST NEARLY
    A. $0.00   B. $23.90   C. $236.10   D. $551.10

21.____

Case Situation No. 2:

Mr. Donald Wilson resides with six dependents in a seven-room unfurnished apartment. Mr. Wilson is employed as an automobile salesman and his gross wages are $4,000 per week. He is employed five days a week and spends $10.00 a day carfare. He spends $50.00 a work day for lunch. His weekly salary deductions are as follows:

    Federal Income Tax $$705.50
    State Income Tax   150.00
    City Income Tax   97.00
    Social Security   301.00
    New York State Disability Insurance   52.50
    Union Due   Not Union Member

22. The weekly amount that Mr. Wilson contributes toward Social Security, New York State Disability Insurance, Federal Income Tax, and Union Dues is MOST NEARLY
    A. $1059.00   B. $1159.00   C. $1306.00   D. $1406.00

22.____

23. The total amount of all weekly expenses incident to Mr. Wilson's employment, which should be deducted from his weekly gross earnings is MOST NEARLY
    A. $1159.00   B. $1306.00   C. $1406.00   D. $1606.00

23.____

24. The semi-monthly family allowance for Mr. Wilson and his six dependents is MOST NEARLY
    A. $2594.00   B. $3205.00   C. $1406.00   D. $4000.00

24.____

25. The semi-monthly amount Mr. Wilson's income available for contribution to his wife and child is MOST NEARLY
    A. $1633.00   B. $2065.40   C. $2594.00   D. $2810.20

25.____

KEY (CORRECT ANSWERS)

1.	D	11.	D
2.	A	12.	B
3.	A	13.	A
4.	C	14.	C
5.	D	15.	D
6.	A	16.	C
7.	C	17.	A
8.	B	18.	B
9.	B	19.	C
10.	A	20.	B

21. A
22. A
23. C
24. C
25. B

EXAMINATION SECTION
TEST 1

DIRECTIONS: Each question or incomplete statement is followed by several suggested answers or completions. Select the one that BEST answers the question or completes the statement. PRINT THE LETTER OF THE CORRECT ANSWER IN THE SPACE AT THE RIGHT.

1. Generally, the MAIN reason for using the questioning technique in a case work interview is to

    A. reveal discrepancies in information given by the client
    B. reinforce your own ideas about the case
    C. obtain necessary factual information about the client
    D. bring out the hidden motives of the client

2. According to a basic case work principle, a worker should "accept" the client, regardless of the client's feelings, attitudes and behavior. This concept of "acceptance" means, most nearly, that the worker

    A. agrees with what the client says, does, and feels
    B. demonstrates his respect for the client as a human being
    C. has no strong opinions about the client's values
    D. thinks the way the client thinks

3. Before visiting a new client, it is desirable for you to be prepared in advance, when possible.
   Which one of the following should generally NOT be included in these advance preparations?

    A. *Learning* as much as possible about the client from the medical chart
    B. *Trying* to put yourself in the client's place
    C. *Recognizing* your own prejudices and stereotypes
    D. *Deciding* on a solution to the client's problems

4. After introducing yourself to a new patient, which one of the following questions generally would be the MOST appropriate for you to ask?

    A. "Do you expect any visitors today?"
    B. "Who is your attending physician?"
    C. "How can I be of help to you?"
    D. "Do you have hospitalization insurance?"

5. In the middle of an interview, a patient makes a statement which seems unclear. Of the following, the BEST way to deal with this situation would be for the worker to

    A. ask the patient to rephrase her statement
    B. rephrase the statement, and ask the patient if that is what she meant
    C. inform the patient that she is not making herself clear
    D. let the patient finish and then try to tie the story together

6. Assume that, at the conclusion of an interview with a client, you have reviewed problems that have been resolved. Generally, the MOST appropriate of the following closing actions for you to take would be to

   A. remind the patient to be on time for the next appointment
   B. go over specific actions that you and the client will take before the next visit
   C. remind the client to take tranquilizers when feeling upset
   D. ask the client to think of new problems to discuss during the next visit

7. Which one of the following would be a MAJOR responsibility of a worker assigned to the surgery ward?

   A. *Instructing* the nurse about changes in medication for patients
   B. *Advising* relatives of the best time to visit patients
   C. *Detecting* anxiety of patients due to their medical illness
   D. *Recording* the number of visitors received by patients

8. Assume that you have been assigned the case of an eight-year-old child whose parents were both seriously injured in an automobile accident. You realize that this child will have severe problems in the months ahead.
   During the *first* interview, of the following, the BEST way to assist the child would be to

   A. convince the child of his ability to be brave and grown-up
   B. play a competitive game with the child and let him win
   C. help the child express his fears and reassure him in accordance with reality
   D. tell the child that his problems are not so great as they may seem

9. Assume that one of your clients has many medical and social problems and needs a good deal of supportive case work help.
   Which one of the following approaches would generally be MOST appropriate for you to use in order to help this client cope with these problems?

   A. *Try* to make the client feel that his problems and situation are unique
   B. *Encourage* the client to be realistic about his situation and assure him that you understand and will do everything possible to help him cope
   C. *Emphasize* to the client those areas you feel you can work on and those which you can do nothing about
   D. *Urge* the client to refrain from taking action on serious matters without asking for your help first

10. Assume that, when you discuss with one of your elderly clients the advisability of applying to the department of socital services for financial assistance, the client becomes extremely upset about the prospect of having to be interviewed by "another stranger."
    Of the following, the BEST way to handle this situation would be to

    A. explain that applying for financial assistance is something the client must do by herself and for herself
    B. offer to accompany the client to social services if necessary, and work with the client toward greater future independence
    C. withdraw your suggestion, since the client's emotional health is your primary consideration
    D. suggest that the client take a personal friend to the interview to help with difficult questions, if necessary

11. Assume that a newspaper reporter calls and questions you regarding the long wait for treatment in the Emergency Room. Of the following, your *MOST* appropriate response would be to

    A. advise the reporter that the long wait is caused by an enormous increase in emergency cases
    B. refer the reporter to the director of social work
    C. tell the reporter that your hospital's emergency room is one of the most efficient in the city
    D. refer the reporter to the hospital employee responsible for public relations

12. When a worker interviews a patient whose problem seems to be typical of that of many other patients she has seen, of the following, it would be *MOST* appropriate to

    A. *attempt* to learn more about the individual circumstances of this patient's situation
    B. *handle* this case the same way as the others were handled
    C. *ask* another worker how she generally handles this type of problem
    D. *reassure* the patient by telling him that many other patients have similar problems

13. A patient without friends or relatives is being discharged from the hospital. He complains to you that his shoes are missing.
    Of the following, your *MOST* appropriate response would be to

    A. advise the patient that this is not a professional concern of yours and suggest that he speak to the ward nurse
    B. advise the patient that he will have to buy a pair of shoes from a nearby shoe store
    C. obtain a pair of shoes for the patient in the hospital clothing room
    D. tell the patient that he probably was not wearing shoes at the time he was admitted

14. The parents of a hospitalized child complain to you that their child is not getting proper nursing care. You have ample opportunity to observe what is happening on the pediatric ward and know that the nurses are extremely conscientious in caring for the children. Your *initial* interpretation of this complaint should be that, probably, the parents

    A. are projecting their anxiety about the child's health by criticizing the nurses
    B. are chronic complainers and must be treated accordingly
    C. may actually want to transfer the child to a more conveniently located hospital
    D. are trying to get special treatment for their child from the nurses

15. You are interviewing an unmarried, attractive young female patient who was in an automobile accident and will not be able to walk again. She says to you: "I'll never find a husband now that I'm crippled."
    In order to help her express her feelings freely, of the following, your *MOST* appropriate response would be:

    A. "You feel that no one will marry you because you can't walk."
    B. "Don't be silly. You have your whole life ahead of you."
    C. "That's not necessarily true. You're young and pretty and smart."
    D. "That may be true, but at least you're alive."

16. Assume that you are in your office completing some paperwork. A man enters and introduces himself as a close friend of one of your patients in the terminal cancer ward. He then asks if he can speak with you, and sits down in the chair next to your desk.
    Of the following, it would be MOST appropriate for you to say FIRST:

    A. "You probably want to know how your friend is coping with his condition."
    B. "You realize, of course, that your friend is dying of cancer."
    C. "What would you like to see me about?"
    D. "What problem would you like to discuss?"

17. During an interview with a new patient your mind wanders momentarily, and you have missed some details in the patient's story.
    Which one of the following would be most appropriate to say FIRST, before the patient continues?

    A. "And then what happened?" – so that the patient will think that you were paying attention all along.
    B. "Could you rephrase that?" – so that the patient will restate the details without being aware of your inattentiveness.
    C. "I'm sorry, I didn't get that, could you repeat that part?" – so that the patient will perceive you as an honest person.
    D. "Please continue". – so that the patient will not have to repeat something that was probably unimportant anyway.

18. Assume that one of your clients is telling you about her family situation. All of a sudden, she says: "Two of my kids go to school, and the third, who is seventeen, ..."
    Then she stops speaking.
    In this situation, of the following, it would be most appropriate for you to FIRST

    A. *state:* "works?"
    B. *state:* "quit school?"
    C. *ask:* "What about the third child?"
    D. *remain silent* for a few seconds

19. You have just started to interview a new client. He begins by telling you that he has been unemployed for the past three years and is receiving almost as much from welfare as he did when he was working. He continues talking along these lines, and then asks you why anybody would want to work when they can be on the dole and maintain almost the same standard of living.
    Of the following, your MOST appropriate response would be:

    A. "I don't personally approve of living in that manner."
    B. "It all depends on a person's values and standards."
    C. "If you are happy living like that, it's all right with me."
    D. "Let's not discuss that. Let's talk about your medical problems first."

20. During your second interview with a young woman, she asks you to drop all this professional stuff and just be friends.
    Which one of the following would be your appropriate response?

    A. "If we were friends, I would probably not be so effective in helping you deal with your problem."
    B. "That's O.K. with me, but you would have to be reassigned to a different worker."
    C. "That would be impossible under the rules and regulations of our agency."
    D. "I really don't think that's appropriate, and I'm a very busy person."

KEY (CORRECT ANSWERS)

1.	C	11.	D
2.	B	12.	A
3.	D	13.	C
4.	C	14.	A
5.	A	15.	A
6.	B	16.	C
7.	C	17.	C
8.	C	18.	D
9.	B	19.	B
10.	B	20.	A

TEST 2

DIRECTIONS: Each question or incomplete statement is followed by several suggested answers or completions, Select the one that BEST answers the question or completes the statement. *PRINT THE LETTER OF THE CORRECT ANSWER IN THE SPACE AT THE RIGHT.*

1. You are interviewing a young man who confides, in you that he is now on probation. In order to help this patient, you decide that it would be desirable to contact his probation officer to obtain additional information.
   Of the following, the BEST way to contact the probation officer would be

   A. *after* the interview, with the patient's consent
   B. *after* the interview, without the patient's consent
   C. *after* the interview, without telling the patient
   D. *during* the interview, with the patient present

2. You introduce yourself to a newly-hospitalized patient and offer to be of assistance if possible. The patient nods that she understands, and begins to discuss her 12-year-old daughter's truancy from school.
   Which one of the following responses would be most appropriate for you to make FIRST?

   A. *I understand your daughter's problem, but can we discuss your problems now?*
   B. *How do you feel this will affect you while you are in the hospital?*
   C. *Did your daughter fail any of her subjects because of her truancy?*
   D. *I have a very large caseload today. Perhaps we can discuss your daughter another time.*

3. You have been interviewing a patient for almost an hour and it is time for your next appointment. As you are about to finish, the patient begins to discuss a new problem.
   In this situation, it would generally be advisable to

   A. close the interview and make another appointment with the patient to discuss this problem
   B. allow the patient to *get things off his chest* before closing the interview
   C. ask the patient why he brought this problem up at the last moment
   D. tell the patient that you cannot discuss this problem because you will be late for your next appointment

4. Assume that you are completing a case involving a deteriorating relationship between the parents of a child who was hospitalized due to an accident caused by the child's father. Since counselling began upon admission of the child, there has been a marked improvement in the relationship between the parents and, in particular, between the child and the father. The child is about to be discharged from the hospital, and you are having an interview with the parents.
   Of the following, according to accepted casework practice, it would be MOST appropriate for you to

   A. assure the parents that, as a result of counselling, they are now *ideal* parents
   B. offer a continuation of counselling until the family's adjustment is stable
   C. review with the parents the *do's and don'ts* of being *good* parents
   D. explain to the parents how you helped them solve their problems

5. Assume that one of your clients, an adult male out-patient who has been coming to see you weekly for four months, fails to keep two appointments. The physician informs you that one of this patient's laboratory tests is positive, indicating the urgent need for follow-up medical care. You have sent the patient a telegram, but he has not replied after a reasonable length of time.
   According to accepted casework practice, of the following, the MOST advisable action for you to take would be to

   A. *contact* a neighbor of the patient and ask the neighbor to persuade the patient to return to the hospital
   B. *inform* a member of the patient's family of the positive; test result and emphasize the urgency of the situation
   C. *write* to the patient and explain the dangers of not returning to the hospital for treatment
   D. *make* an emergency visit to the patient at home and tell him about the positive test result and the importance of returning to the hospital

6. Assume that you are trying to establish the identity of an elderly woman who was brought to the Emergency Room by the police, who found her on the street, somewhat disoriented. The doctor decides to admit the woman, whose blood pressure is elevated, and who has an open ulcerated wound on her leg. She is very talkative about events long in the past, can't recall where she lives, but keeps speaking of having to *go home to give her sister breakfast*. The police have found that she has a card giving her name and an address which is three blocks from the hospital, but the telephone company has no listing for her.
   Of the following, your MOST advisable action would be to

   A. ask the hospital security guards to make a visit to the address on the card and tell any relatives of the woman that she is hospitalized
   B. have a visiting nurse make a visit to the address and check on the sister's possible need for food and medical attention
   C. call the social service exchange to determine whether the woman is known to any agency and what information they may have about her and her sister
   D. make a visit to the address on the card in order to obtai more information about the woman

7. You are a worker assigned to the alcoholism clinic. One of your clients appears for an interview in an intoxicated condition. Of the following, your MOST appropriate action would be to

   A. discuss the patient's drinking problem with him in no uncertain terms
   B. make another appointment and point out to the patient that he cannot be interviewed while intoxicated
   C. threaten to close the case and discharge the patient if he does not sober up
   D. recommend psychological testing to determine why the patient persists in drinking in spite of counselling

8. As a worker in the family planning clinic, you are counselling an 18-year-old unmarried patient who is pregnant. She is in a state of conflict, because she wants an abortion, but her boyfriend is encouraging her to marry him and bear the child.
Of the following, your MOST appropriate action would be to

   A. ask the patient why she was careless after receiving guidance from the family planning clinic
   B. encourage the patient to make the decision for herself, and Be supportive of her choice
   C. stress the positive qualities of her boyfriend, who is offering to marry her
   D. determine whether the conflict may derive from the patient's religious upbringing

9. Assume that one of your cases, a woman who has given birth three days ago, is now verbally abusive to the staff, and refuses to see her infant. Of the following, your MOST appropriate course of action would be to

   A. scold the woman for her childish behavior
   B. attempt to convince the woman that once she sees the baby she will feel much better
   C. speak with the woman in an effort to understand her behavior
   D. tell the woman that she will be transferred to the psychiatric unit if she does not behave

10. Assume that you are interviewing an unmarried female patient in the Emergency Room. The doctor has just told her that she must be admitted to the hospital on an emergency basis, but she refuses to accept this recommendation because she has three small children, has no one to care for them, and does not want to leave them alone.
Of the following, the most appropriate action for you to take FIRST would be to

   A. suggest that the patient try to enlist neighbors to help look after the children
   B. ask the doctor to admit the children with their mother on an emergency basis
   C. try to locate the children's father and ask him to look after the children
   D. explain to the patient that it is possible for you to arrange for care of the children

11. Assume that you are assigned to the methadone maintenance clinic. As you are about to finish an interview, your client asks you to lend him ten dollars. Of the following, your most appropriate FIRST action would be to

   A. inform the client that it is against hospital policy for a worker to lend money to a patient
   B. lend the client the ten dollars
   C. suggest that the client borrow the money from a personal friend
   D. advise the client to apply to the department of social services for an emergency grant

12. You are interviewing a young unmarried woman who is pregnant, says that she is not sure she can care for her baby properly, and is considering requesting an abortion. Of the following, your MOST appropriate response would be:

   A. *What do you think of as proper care for your baby?*
   B. *I'm sure you will be an excellent mother.*
   C. *Do you know who the father is?*
   D. *How long have you been pregnant?*

13. You are interviewing a married patient with two young children with regard to her impending surgery. Suddenly, she asks if you are married. Of the following, the MOST appropriate response would be to tell her

    A. whether you are married, and then ask why she wants to know
    B. you are not now married, but that you are engaged to be married
    C. this is irrelevant, and continue discussing her situation
    D. you used to be married, but that you are now divorced

14. You are visiting a new patient on your assigned ward. After introducing yourself and offering to be of assistance, the patient begins to tell you a lengthy story relating to her illness. According to accepted interviewing techniques, of the following, it would be MOST appropriate for you to indicate your concern and interest by

    A. briefly commenting or asking questions, indicating that you are grasping the essential points
    B. saying nothing, so as not to interrupt the patient's train of thought
    C. interrupting frequently to clarify points you do not fully comprehend
    D. asking the patient to pause at periodic intervals so that you may proceed to ask structured questions

15. You have been counseling an adult patient on the cancer ward on a weekly basis for about a month and it is now time to decide where the patient will live after being discharged from the hospital.
    According to accepted practice, the FINAL decision on this matter should be made by

    A. you, the case worker
    B. the patient's relatives
    C. the patient, with the case worker's help
    D. the patient and the doctors

16. Assume that a patient in your caseload asks you for specific advice regarding his unhappy marital situation. In deciding whether to respond to this request, you should generally consider all of the following EXCEPT

    A. any possible underlying anxiety the patient may have
    B. the patient's ability to carry out the advice
    C. the seriousness of the patient's situation
    D. whether the client will accept or reject your advice

17. According to accepted casework practice, when interviewing a young child it is considered especially important for the worker to closely observe the child's behavior, feelings, and mood, in addition to listening to what the child says, MAINLY because such observation should

    A. provide significant diagnostic information about the child
    B. help the child feel closer to the worker
    C. enable the worker to sense the right time to console the child
    D. give the worker clues as to when to humor the child

18. You find it necessary to refer a client for psychiatric help upon discharge. The client consents to this plan, but asks you to omit from your report certain information he has told you in confidence. You feel that the psychiatrist's knowledge of this information would be of great benefit in helping your client.
    For you to go ahead and include this information in your report to the psychiatrist, without the client's consent, would be considered

    A. *good practice*, because the psychiatrist will need all available information about the client
    B. *bad practice*, because this action would be a breach of confidence
    C. *good practice*, because helping the client is the primary goal of case work
    D. *bad practice*, because the patient would probably find out eventually that this information was disclosed

19. You are interviewing a woman who has suffered a severe beating from her husband, is obviously upset, and embarrassed about having to relate the details to you.
    Of the following, the MOST appropriate way for you to handle this situation would be to

    A. insist that she tell you the whole story, including the details
    B. postpone discussion of the beating until the woman feels better
    C. tell the woman to omit the details for now, and ask her how you can be of help
    D. postpone this interview until the husband is available to present his side of the story

20. You are making discharge plans for an alert, 78-year-old retired school teacher who is recovering satisfactorily from a minor operation. One day, when you come to her room, she fails to recognize you and tells you disconnected stories about people she knew in childhood.
    Of the following, the MOST appropriate way to handle this changed situation would be to

    A. tell the patient she had better *snap out of it*
    B. advise the patient that you will return when she starts talking sense
    C. confer with the attending physician about this change in the patient's condition
    D. suggest to the physician that the discharge plan be changed to recommend admission to a State hospital

KEY (CORRECT ANSWERS)

1.	A	11.	A
2.	B	12.	A
3.	A	13.	A
4.	B	14.	A
5.	D	15.	C
6.	D	16.	D
7.	B	17.	A
8.	B	18.	B
9.	C	19.	C
10.	D	20.	C

EXAMINATION SECTION

TEST 1

DIRECTIONS: Each question or incomplete statement is followed by several suggested answers or completions. Select the one that BEST answers the question or completes the statement. *PRINT THE LETTER OF THE CORRECT ANSWER IN THE SPACE AT THE RIGHT.*

1. The PRIMARY function of the Department of Social Services is to
    A. refer needy persons to legally responsible relatives for support
    B. enable needy persons to become self-supporting
    C. refer ineligible persons to private agencies
    D. grant aid to needy eligible persons
    E. administer public assistance programs in which the federal and state governments do not participate

   1.____

2. A public assistance program objective should be designed to
    A. provide for eligible persons in accordance with their individual requirements and with consideration of the circumstances in which they live
    B. provide for eligible persons at a standard of living equal to that enjoyed while they were self-supporting
    C. make sure that assistance payments from public funds are not too liberal
    D. guard against providing a better living for persons receiving aid than is enjoyed by the most frugal independent families
    E. eliminate the need for private welfare agencies

   2.____

3. It is often stated that it would be better to abolish the need for relief rather than to extend the existing public assistance programs.
   This statement suggests that
    A. existing legislation makes it too easy for people to apply for and receive assistance
    B. public assistance should be limited to institutional care for rehabilitative purposes
    C. the support of needy persons should be the responsibility of their own families and relatives rather than that of the government
    D. the existing criteria used to determine *need* for public assistance are too liberal and should be modified to include a *work* test
    E. attempts should be made to eradicate those forces in our social organization which cause poverty

   3.____

4. The one of the following types of public assistance which is frequently described as a *special privilege* is
    A. veteran assistance
    B. emergency assistance
    C. aid to dependent children
    D. old-age assistance
    E. vocational rehabilitation of the handicapped

   4.____

5. The principle of *settlement* holds that each community is responsible for the care of its own members and that communities should not bear the costs of care for needy non-residents.
This was an intrinsic principle of the
   A. English Poor Laws
   B. Home Rule Amendment
   C. Single Tax Proposal
   D. National Bankruptcy Regulations
   E. Proportional Representation Act

5.____

6. The FIRST form of state social security legislation developed in the United States was
   A. health insurance
   B. unemployment compensation
   C. workmen's compensation
   D. old-age insurance
   E. old-age assistance

6.____

7. The plan for establishing a federal department with Cabinet status to be known as the Department of Health, Education, and Welfare, was
   A. vetoed by the President after having been passed by Congress
   B. disapproved by the Senate after having been passed by the House of Representatives
   C. rejected by both the Senate and the House of Representatives
   D. enacted into legislation during a past session of Congress
   E. determined to be unconstitutional

7.____

8. Census Bureau reports show certain definite social trends in our population. One of these trends which was a major contributing factor in the establishment of the federal old-age insurance system was the
   A. increased rate of immigration to the United States
   B. rate at which the number of Americans living to 65 years of age and beyond is increasing
   C. increasing amounts spent for categorical relief in the country as a whole
   D. decreasing number of legally responsible relatives who have been unable to assist the aged since the Depression of 1929
   E. number of states which have failed to meet their obligations in the care of the aged

8.____

9. The Federal Housing Administration is the agency which
   A. insures mortgages made by lending institutions for new construction or remodeling of old construction
   B. provides federal aid for state and local governments for slum clearance and housing for very low income families
   C. subsidizes the building industry through direct grants
   D. provides for the construction of low-cost housing projects owned and operated by the federal government
   E. combines city planning with government subsidies for large-scale housing

9.____

10. Reports show that more men than women are physically handicapped MAINLY because
    A. women are instinctively more cautious than men
    B. men are more likely to have congenital deformities
    C. women tend to see surgical remedies because of greater concern over personal appearance
    D. men have lower ability to recover from injury
    E. men are more likely to be exposed to hazardous conditions

11. Of the following, the explanation married women give MOST frequently for seeking employment outside the home is that they wish to
    A. escape the drudgeries of home life
    B. develop secondary employment skills
    C. maintain an emotionally satisfying career
    D. provide the main support for the family
    E. supplement the family income

12. Of the following home conditions, the one MOST likely to cause emotional disturbances in children is
    A. increased birthrate following the war
    B. disrupted family relationships
    C. lower family income than that of neighbors
    D. higher family income than that of neighbors
    E. overcrowded living conditions

13. Casual unemployment, as distinguished from other types of unemployment, is traceable MOST readily to
    A. a decrease in the demand for labor as a result of scientific progress
    B. more or less haphazard changes in the demand for labor in certain industries
    C. periodic changes in the demand for labor in certain industries
    D. disturbances and disruptions in industry resulting from international trade barriers
    E. increased mobility of the population

14. Labor legislation, although primarily intended for the benefit of the employee, may aid the employer by
    A. increasing his control over the immediate labor market
    B. prohibiting government interference with operating policies
    C. protecting him, through equalization of labor costs, from being undercut by other employers
    D. transferring to the general taxpayer the principal costs of industrial hazards of accident and unemployment
    E. increasing the pensions of civil service employees

15. When employment and unemployment figures both decline, the MOST probable conclusion is that
    A. the population has reached a condition of equilibrium
    B. seasonal employment has ended

C. the labor force has decreased
D. payments for unemployment insurance have been increased
E. industrial progress has reduced working hours

16. In evaluating the adequacy of an individual's income, a social service worker should place primary emphasis on
    A. its value in relation to the average income
    B. the source of the income
    C. its relation to the earning capacity of the individual
    D. its purchasing power
    E. the purposes for which it is spent

    16.____

17. An individual with an I.Q. of 100 may be said to have demonstrated _____ intelligence.
    A. superior
    B. absolute
    C. substandard
    D. approximately average
    E. high average

    17.____

18. While state legislatures differ in many respects, all of them are MOST NEARLY alike in
    A. provisions for retirement of members
    B. rate of pay
    C. length of legislative sessions
    D. method of selection of their members
    E. length of term of office

    18.____

19. If a state passed a law in a field under Congressional jurisdiction and if Congress subsequently passed contrary legislation, the state provision would be
    A. regarded as never having existed
    B. valid until the next session of the state legislature which would be obliged to repeal it
    C. superseded by the federal statute
    D. ratified by Congress
    E. still operative in the state involved

    19.____

20. Power to pardon offenses committed against the people of the United States is vested in the
    A. Supreme Court of the United States
    B. United States District Courts
    C. Federal Bureau of Investigation
    D. United States Parole Board
    E. President of the United States

    20.____

21. As distinguished from formal social control of an individual's behavior, an example of informal social control is that exerted by
    A. public opinion
    B. religious doctrine
    C. educational institutions
    D. statutes
    E. public health measures

    21.____

22. The PRINCIPAL function of the jury in a jury trial is to decide questions of 22.____
    A. equity   B. fact   C. injunction
    D. contract   D. law

23. Of the following rights of an individual, the one which usually depends on citizenship as distinguished from those given anyone living under the laws of the United States is the right to 23.____
    A. receive public assistance
    B. hold an elective office
    C. petition the government for redress of grievances
    D. receive equal protection of the laws
    E. be accorded a trial by jury

24. The name of Thomas Malthus is MOST closely associated with a work on 24.____
    A. population   B. political justice   C. capitalism
    D. social contract E. wealth of nations

25. A chronic functional disease characterized by fits or attacks in which there is a loss of consciousness with a succession of convulsions is called 25.____
    A. epilepsy   B. dipsomania   C. catalepsy
    D. Hodgkin's disease E. paresis

KEY (CORRECT ANSWERS)

1.	D		11.	E
2.	A		12.	B
3.	E		13.	B
4.	A		14.	C
5.	A		15.	C
6.	C		16.	D
7.	D		17.	D
8.	B		18.	D
9.	A		19.	C
10.	E		20.	E

21. A
22. B
23. B
24. A
25. A

TEST 2

DIRECTIONS: Each question or incomplete statement is followed by several suggested answers or completions. Select the one that BEST answers the question or completes the statement. *PRINT THE LETTER OF THE CORRECT ANSWER IN THE SPACE AT THE RIGHT.*

Questions 1-10.

DIRECTIONS: Questions 1 through 10, inclusive, are based on the following table, which gives a partial summary of certain groups of cases in the social services center of a public assistance agency.

SOCIAL SERVICES CENTER CASELOAD SUMMARY, JUNE-SEPTEMBER

	June	July	August	September
Total Cases Under Care at End of Month	13,790	11,445	13,191	12,209
Home relief	4,739	2,512	6,055	5,118
Old-age assistance	5,337	b	5,440	2,265
Aid to dependent children	3,487	1,621	1,520	4,594
Aid to the Blind	227	251	176	232
Net Change During Month	-344	c	1,746	-982
Applications Made During Month	1,542	789	3,153	1,791
Total Cases Accepted during Month	534	534	2,879	982
Home relief	278	213	342	338
Old-age assistance	43	161	1,409	f
Aid to dependent children	195	153	1,115	307
Aid to the blind	18	7	13	14
Total Cases Closed During Month	878	d	1,133	1,964
To private employment	326	1,197	460	870
To unemployment insurance	96	421	126	205
Reclassified	176	326	178	399
All other reasons	280	935	e	490
Total Cases Carried Over to Next Month	a	11,445	13,191	12,209

1. The number which should be placed in the blank indicated by *a* is 1.____
   A. 12,912   B. 13,446   C. 13,790
   D. 14,134   E. None of the above

2. The number which should be placed in the blank indicated by *b* is 2.____
   A. 6,385   B. 7,601   C. 8,933
   D. 7,061   E. None of the above

3. The number which should be placed in the blank indicated by *c* is 3.____
   A. -2,345   B. -344   C. 344
   D. 3,413   E. None of the above

2 (#2)

4. The number which should be placed in the blank indicated by *d* is
   A. 2,789   B. 2,345   C. 7,601
   D. 3,879   E. None of the above

   4._____

5. Of the total number of cases closed during the month of August, the percentage closed for reasons other than reclassification or receipt of unemployment insurance is APPROXIMATELY
   A. 13.8%   B. 73.17%   C. 26.83%   D. 40.60%   E. 24.63%

   5._____

6. In comparing June and July, the figures indicate that with respect to the total cases under care at the end of each month,
   A. the percentage of total cases accepted during the month was lower in June
   B. the percentage of total cases accepted during the month was higher in June
   C. the percentage of total cases accepted during both months was the same
   D. there were more cases under care at the end of July
   E. there is insufficient data for comparison of the total cases under care at the end of each month

   6._____

7. The total number of cases accepted during the entire period in the category in which most cases were accepted was
   A. 1,409   B. 1,936   C. 1,770   D. 4,929   E. 20,103

   7._____

8. In comparing July and September, the figures indicate that
   A. more cases were closed in September because of private employment
   B. the total number of cases accepted during the month consisted of a greater proportion of home relief cases in September
   C. in one of these months, there were more total cases under care at the end of the month than at the beginning of the month
   D. aid to dependent children cases at the beginning of September numbered almost three times as many as at the beginning of July
   E. none of the above is correct

   8._____

9. The total number of applications made during the four-month period was
   A. more than four times the number of cases closed because of private employment during the same period
   B. less than the combined totals of aid to dependent children cases under care in June and July
   C. 4,376 more than the total number of cases accepted during August
   D. 23 times as large as the number of cases reclassified in July
   E. 5,916 less than the total number of cases carried over to September

   9._____

10. The ratio of old-age assistance cases accepted in August to the total number of such cases under care at the end of that month is expressed with the GREATEST degree of accuracy by the figures
    A. 1:4   B. 1:25   C. 4:1   D. 7:128   E. 10:39

    10._____

11. The term *mores* refers to
    A. English meadows B. bribery C. Moorish worship
    D. telegraphic code E. social customs

12. *Disparity* refers MOST directly to
    A. difference B. argument C. low wages
    D. separation E. injustice

13. The technical term used to express the ratio between mental and chronological age is called the
    A. mentality rating B. culture level index
    C. psychometric standard D. achievement index
    E. intelligence quotient

14. In social services work, the disorganizing factors in a personal or familial situation which prevent or hinder rehabilitation are called
    A. median deviations B. transference situations
    C. rank correlations D. liabilities
    E. collective representations

15. The period in the life of man when mental abilities begin to deteriorate is known as
    A. puberty B. adolescence C. gerontology
    D. senility E. antiquity

Questions 16-25.

DIRECTIONS: Questions 16 through 25, inclusive, contain two blank spaces each. You are to select the words which will fill the blanks so that the sentence will be true and sensible. For the *first* blank in each question, select a word or phrase preceded by letter A, B, C, D, or E. For the *second* blank in the question, select a word or phrase preceded by letter V, W, X, Y, or Z. Use the two letters you have selected as your answer and print both these letters in the correspondingly numbered space at the right.

16. _____ is to public assistance as citizenship is to _____.
    A. need B. school attendance C. worthiness
    D. child E. welfare center
    V. passport W. alien X. immigration
    Y. excise tax Z. indictment

17. _____ is to home relief as public institutional care is to _____.
    A. compensation B. supplementation
    C. direct relief D. survivor's insurance
    E. fiscal period
    V. removal of custody W. adoption
    X. indoor relief Y. day care
    Z. voucher assistance

18. _____ is to face sheet as income is to _____.
    A. client   B. cash relief
    C. relief standard   D. case record
    E. emergency assistance
    V. wages   W. home
    X. debts   Y. taxes
    Z. bonus

19. _____ is to demography as man is to _____.
    A. politics   B. racial relations   C. stigmata
    D. social statistics   E. democracy
    V. population   W. geography   X. woman
    Y. marriage   Z. anthropology

20. _____ is to tuberculosis as Terman is to _____.
    A. Wasserman   B. Mantoux   C. Schick
    D. Ascheim-Zondek   E. Snellen
    V. litmus test   W. means test   X. lie detector test
    Y. intelligence test   Z. CAVD test

21. _____ is to dementia as feeblemindedness is to _____.
    A. anger   B. luxation   C. insanity
    D. diagnosis   E. psychiatry
    V. myopia   W. amentia   X. tibia
    Y. criminal   Z. childhood

22. Frustration is to _____ as _____ is to relaxation.
    A. satisfaction   B. goal   C. need
    D. desire   E. motive
    V. tension   W. behavior   X. adjustment
    Y. readjustment   Z. reaction

23. _____ is to embezzlement as parole is to _____.
    A. intent   B. larceny   C. desertion
    D. guilt   E. conviction
    V. bail   W. plea   X. probation
    Y. innocence   Z. reformatory

24. Abandonment is to _____ as coercion is to _____.
    A. abduction   B. discovery   C. guardian
    D. adultery   E. desertion
    V. desertion   W. impotence   X. crime
    Y. coition   Z. constraint

25. _____ is to homicide as felony is to _____.
    A. courthouse   B. mayhem   C. negligence
    D. witness   E. manslaughter
    V. judge   W. crime   X. autopsy
    Y. civil suit   Z. prosecutor

KEY (CORRECT ANSWERS)

1.	C		11.	E
2.	D		12.	A
3.	A		13.	E
4.	E		14.	D
5.	B		15.	D
6.	A		16.	AV
7.	B		17.	CX
8.	E		18.	DV
9.	E		19.	DZ
10.	E		20.	BY

21. CW
22. AV
23. BX
24. EZ
25. EW

TEST 3

DIRECTIONS: Each question or incomplete statement is followed by several suggested answers or completions. Select the one that BEST answers the question or completes the statement. *PRINT THE LETTER OF THE CORRECT ANSWER IN THE SPACE AT THE RIGHT.*

Questions 1-3.

DIRECTIONS: Questions 1 through 3, inclusive, are to be answered on the basis of the following passage.

Aid to dependent children shall be given to a parent or other relative as herein specified for the benefit of a child or children under sixteen years of age or of a minor or minors between sixteen and eighteen years of age if in the judgment of the administrative agency: (1) the granting of an allowance will be in the interest of such child or minor, and (2) the parent or other relative is a fit person to bring up such child or minor so that his physical, mental, and moral well-being will be safeguarded, and (3) aid is necessary to enable such parent or other relative to do so, and (4) such child or minor is a resident of the state on the date of application for aid, and (5) such minor between sixteen and eighteen years of age is regularly attending school in accordance with the regulations of the department. An allowance may be granted for the aid of such child or minor who has been deprived or parental support or care by reason of the death, continued absence from the home, or physical or mental incapacity of a parent, and who is living with his father, mother, grandfather, grandmother, brother, sister, stepfather, stepmother, stepbrother, stepsister, uncle or aunt. In making such allowances, consideration shall be given to the ability of the relative making application and of any other relatives to support and care for or to contribute to the support and care of such child or minor. In making all such allowances, it shall be made certain that the religious faith of the child or minor shall be preserved and protected.

1. The preceding passage is concerned PRIMARILY with
   A. the financial ability of persons applying for public assistance
   B. compliance on the part of applicants with the *settlement* provisions of the law
   C. the fitness of parents or other relatives to bring up physically, mentally, or morally delinquent children between the ages of sixteen and eighteen
   D. eligibility for aid to dependent children
   E. the religious faith of children or minors coming within the provisions of this law

2. On the basis of the preceding passage, the MOST accurate of the following statements is:
   A. Mary Doe, mother of John, age 18, is entitled to aid for her son if he is attending school regularly
   B. Evelyn Stowe, mother of Eleanor, age 13, is not entitled to aid for Eleanor if she uses her home for immoral purposes
   C. Ann Roe, cousin of Helen, age 14, is entitled to aid for Helen if the latter is living with her
   D. Peter Moe, uncle of Henry, age 15, is not entitled to aid for Henry if the latter is living with him

1.____

2.____

E. Harriet Hoe, mother of Paul, age 7, is not entitled to aid for him if she has been divorced from her husband

3. The above passage is PROBABLY an excerpt of the
   A. Administrative Code
   B. Social Welfare Law
   C. Federal Security Act
   D. City Charter
   E. Colonial Laws of the state

4. Recent amendment of the Social Security Act has produced major changes in the administration of public assistance.
   The one of the following which is NOT included among these changes is the
   A. availability of federal funds in matching payments for home relief to veterans who are employable but unemployed
   B. establishment of federal grants-in-aid for a category of assistance to be known as aid to the permanently and totally disabled
   C. extension of the four categories of assistance to Puerto Rico and the Virgin Islands
   D. sharing by the federal government of costs of assistance to needy aged and blind persons in public medical institutions
   E. availability of federal funds within present federal maxima in matching indirect payments for medical care in old-age assistance, aid to the blind, and aid to dependent children

5. The length of residence required to make a person eligible for the various forms of public assistance available in the United States
   A. is the same in all states but is different among public assistance programs in a given state
   B. is the same in all states and among different public assistance programs in a given state
   C. is the same in all states for different categories
   D. varies among states and among different public assistance programs in a given state
   E. varies only in the local agencies of a given state

6. The Social Welfare Law requires that whenever an applicant for aid to dependent children resides in a place where there is a central index or a social service exchange, the public welfare official shall register the case with such index or exchange.
   This requirement is for the purpose of
   A. preventing duplication and coordinating the work of public and private agencies
   B. establishing prior claims on the amounts of assistance furnished when repayments are made
   C. having the social service exchange determine which agency should handle the case
   D. providing statistical data regarding the number of persons receiving grants for aid to dependent children
   E. making sure that opportunities for private employment are available to persons receiving assistance

7. A person who knowingly brings a needy person from another state into the state for the purpose of making him a public charge, is guilty of
   A. violation of the Displaced Persons Act
   B. violation of the Mann Act
   C. a felony
   D. a misdemeanor
   E. no offense

   7._____

8. Among the following needy persons, the one NOT eligible to receive veteran assistance is the
   A. husband of a veteran, if living with the veteran
   B. minor grandchild of a veteran, if living with the veteran
   C. incapacitated child of a deceased veteran
   D. stepmother of stepfather of a veteran, if living with the veteran
   E. non-veteran brother or sister of a veteran, if living with the veteran

   8._____

9. The term *state residence*, as defined in the Social Welfare Law, means continuous residence within the state for a period of AT LEAST
   A. one year   B. two years   C. six months
   D. one month   E. one day

   9._____

10. In order to be eligible for old-age assistance in this state, applicants must have resided continuously in the state prior to the date of application for
    A. three months   B. six months   C. one year
    D. five years   E. no specific period

    10._____

11. Under the Social Security Act, public assistance payments do NOT provide for
    A. old-age assistance
    B. care of children in foster homes
    C. aid to the blind
    D. aid to dependent children
    E. aid to the permanently and totally disabled

    11._____

12. The Social Welfare Law provides that certain relatives of a recipient of public assistance or care, or of a person liable to become in need thereof, be responsible for the support of such person if they are of sufficient ability. The one of the following who is NOT a legally responsible relative is a(n)
    A. mother
    B. child
    C. grandparent
    D. uncle
    E. step-parent, for a minor stepchild

    12._____

13. Of the following, the distinguishing characteristics of a *dependent child* as defined in the Social Welfare Law, refer to a child who is
    A. in the custody of, or wholly or partly maintained by an authorized organization of charitable, eleemosynary, correctional, or reformatory character

    13._____

B. in such condition of want or suffering or who under improper guardianship as to injure or endanger the morals of himself or others
C. between 16 and 18 years of age and solely dependent upon his parents for support and maintenance
D. under 16 years of age and deserted or abandoned by parents or other persons lawfully charged with his care
E. incorrigible or ungovernable and beyond the control of his parents or guardian

14. Recent adoption laws tend to place increased emphasis upon 14.____
    A. informal signing of adoption papers
    B. lowered residence requirements for adoption
    C. establishment of the child's inheritance rights
    D. social investigation of the home before adoption
    E. increased boarding rates paid to adoptive parents

15. Any person or organization soliciting donations in public places is required to have a license issued by the 15.____
    A. Police Department   B. Department of Sanitation
    C. Division of Labor Relations   D. Department of Social Services
    E. Department of Licenses

16. A person who, though himself, in good health, harbors disease germs which may be passed on to others, is called a(n) 16.____
    A. instigator   B. carrier   C. incubator
    D. inoculator   E. malingerer

17. Diseases most commonly caused by certain working environments or conditions are known as _____ diseases. 17.____
    A. infectious   B. contagious   C. occupational
    D. hereditary   E. compensatory

18. The process of destroying micro-organisms which cause disease or infection is called 18.____
    A. contamination   B. immunization C. inoculation
    D. sterilization   E. infestation

19. Proper utilization of the term *carious* would involve reference to 19.____
    A. teeth
    B. curiosity
    C. shipment of food packages to needy persons in Europe
    D. hazardous or precarious situations
    E. lack of reasonable precautions

20. The chemical agent which has been used extensively to prevent the spread of typhus infection is 20.____
    A. cortisone   B. D.D.T.   C. penicillin
    D. ephedrine   E. sulfanilamide

21. The medical term for *hardening of the arteries* is
    A. carcinoma   B. arthritis   C. thrombosis
    D. arteriosclerosis   E. phlebitis

    21._____

22. A set of symptoms which occur together is called a
    A. sympathin   B. syncope   C. syndrome
    D. synecdoche   E. syllogism

    22._____

23. If the characteristics of a person were being studied by competent observers, it would be expected that their observations would differ MOST markedly with respect to their evaluation of the person's
    A. intelligence   B. nutritional characteristics
    C. temperamental characteristics   D. weight
    E. height

    23._____

24. If there are evidences of dietary deficiency in families where cereals make up a major portion of the diet, the MOST likely reason for this deficiency is that
    A. cereals cause absorption of excessive quantities of water
    B. persons who concentrate their diet on cereals do not chew their food properly
    C. carbohydrates are deleterious
    D. other essential food elements are omitted
    E. children eat cereals too rapidly

    24._____

25. Although malnutrition is generally associated with poverty, dietary studies of population groups in the United States reveal that
    A. malnutrition is most often due to a deficiency of nutrients found chiefly in high-cost foods
    B. there has been overemphasis of the causal relationship between poverty and malnutrition
    C. malnutrition is found among people with sufficient money to be well fed
    D. a majority of the population in all income groups is undernourished
    E. malnutrition is not a factor in the incidence of rickets

    25._____

KEY (CORRECT ANSWERS)

1.	D		11.	B
2.	B		12.	D
3.	B		13.	A
4.	A		14.	D
5.	D		15.	D
6.	A		16.	B
7.	D		17.	C
8.	E		18.	D
9.	A		19.	A
10.	E		20.	B

21. D
22. C
23. C
24. D
25. C

TEST 4

DIRECTIONS: Each question or incomplete statement is followed by several suggested answers or completions. Select the one that BEST answers the question or completes the statement. *PRINT THE LETTER OF THE CORRECT ANSWER IN THE SPACE AT THE RIGHT.*

1. A medically trained person who treats mental diseases is called a(n) 1.____
   A. psychologist   B. sociologist   C. psychiatrist
   D. physiologist   E. opthamologist

2. Of the following social agencies, the which must rely MOST on short-contact interviewing is the 2.____
   A. child-guidance clinic   B. Travelers' Aid Society
   C. Social Service Exchange   D. Hospital for Crippled Children
   E. juvenile court

3. The organization which has as one of its primary functions the mitigation of suffering caused by famine, fire, floods, and other national calamities is the 3.____
   A. National Safety Council   B. Salvation Army
   C. Public Administration Services D. American National Red Cross
   E. American Legion

4. The MAIN difference between public welfare and private social agencies is that in public agencies 4.____
   A. case records are open to the public
   B. the granting of assistance cannot be sufficiently flexible to meet the varying needs of individual recipients
   C. only financial assistance may be provided
   D. all policies and procedures must be based upon statutory authorizations
   E. economical and efficient administration are stressed because their funds are obtained through public taxation

5. Proper handling of a case in which the applicant requires temporary congregate care would involve a referral initially to 5.____
   A. a private agency   B. a religious institution
   C. the state welfare agency D. the federal government
   E. one of the municipal shelters

6. A recipient of relief who is in need of the services on an attorney but is unable to pay the customary fees, should generally be referred to the 6.____
   A. Small Claims Court   B. Domestic Relations Court
   C. County Lawyers Association D. City Law Department
   E. Legal Aid Society

7. A person who is not satisfied with the action taken by the Department of Social Services on his application for old-age assistance may appeal to the State Department of Social Welfare for an impartial review and a *fair hearing*. 7.____

97

2 (#4)

The final decision in such a hearing is made by the
- A. State Board of Social Welfare
- B. State Commissioner of Social Welfare
- C. Commissioner of Social Services
- D. Attorney-General of the State
- E. Federal Security Agency

8. An injured worker should file his claim for workmen's compensation with the   8.____
    - A. State Labor Relations Board
    - B. Division of Placement and Unemployment Insurance
    - C. State Industrial Commission
    - D. Workmen's Compensation Board
    - E. State Insurance Board

9. In order to supplement the care and guidance furnished to young people by   9.____
   the family and other social institutions, the legislature created a temporary
   agency known as the State Youth Commission.
   Among the powers and duties of this Commission are those listed below, with
   the EXCEPTION of
    - A. supervising the administration of state institutions for juvenile delinquents
    - B. authorizing payment of state aid to municipalities in accordance with the provisions of the Youth Commission Act
    - C. making studies and recommendations regarding the guidance and treatment of juvenile delinquents
    - D. devising plans for the creation and operation of youth bureaus and recreation projects
    - E. making necessary studies and analyses of the problems of youth guidance and the prevention of juvenile delinquency

10. One of the institutions operated by the State Department of Social Welfare is   10.____
    the
    - A. State School for the Blind, Batavia
    - B. State Training School for Boys, Warwick
    - C. State Reconstruction Home, West Haverstraw
    - D. State School for Mental Defectives, Newark
    - E. Woodbourne Institute for Defective Delinquents, Woodbourne

11. The one of the following which is NOT included among the responsibilities of   11.____
    the Bureau of Public Assistance of the Social Security Administration is
    - A. reviewing and approving state plans for public assistance and the operation of these plans, in order to determine their continuing conformity to the Social Security Act
    - B. administering provisions for grants by the federal government to states for old-age assistance, aid to the blind, aid to dependent children, and aid to the permanently and totally disabled
    - C. carrying out the Social Security Administration's functions in connection with the federal-state unemployment insurance system

D. reviewing state estimates for public assistance and certifying the amount of federal grants to states
E. collecting, analyzing, and publishing data on the operation of all forms of public assistance in the states, including general assistance

12. Because of the number of able-bodied employable persons on relief, the Department of Social Services once adopted the policy of
    A. removing all employables from the relief rolls
    B. subjecting such persons to special review in order to determine whether they are concealing facts about employment
    C. assigning such persons to various city departments for appropriate employment commensurate with the amount of relief grants
    D. forcing all men on the employable list to apply to other governmental agencies as provisional civil service workers
    E. requesting selective service boards to give preference to such employable persons of appropriate age for induction into the armed forces

12.____

13. The type of insurance found MOST frequently among families such as those assisted by the Department of Social Services is
    A. accident   B. straight life   C. endowment
    D. industrial   E. personal liability

13.____

14. Of the following items in the standard budget of the Department of Social Services, the one for which actual expenditures would be MOST constant throughout the year is
    A. fuel   B. housing
    C. medical care   D. clothing
    E. household replacements

14.____

15. The MOST frequent cause of *broken homes* is attributed to the
    A. temperamental incompatibilities of parents and in-laws
    B. extension of the system of children's courts
    C. psychopathic irresponsibility of the parents
    D. institutionalization of one of the spouses
    E. death of one or both spouses

15.____

16. In rearing children, the problems of the widower are usually greater than those of the widow, largely because of the
    A. tendency of widowers to impose excessively rigid moral standards
    B. increased economic hardship
    C. added difficulty of maintaining a desirable home
    D. possibility that a stepmother will be added to the household
    E. prevalent masculine prejudice against pursuits which are inherently feminine

16.____

17. Foster-home placement of children is often advocated in preference to institutionalization PRIMARILY because
    A. the law does not provide for local supervision of children's institutions
    B. institutions furnish a more expensive type of care
    C. the number of institutions is insufficient compared to the number of children needing car
    D. children are not well treated in institutions
    E. foster homes provide a more normal environment for children

18. Of the following, the category MOST likely to yield the greatest reduction in cost to the taxpayer under improved employment conditions is
    A. home relief, including aid to the homeless
    B. aid to the blind
    C. aid to dependent children
    D. old-age assistance
    E. aid to the permanently and totally disabled

19. One of the MOST common characteristics of the chronic alcoholic is
    A. low intelligence level
    B. wanderlust
    C. psychosis
    D. independence
    E. egocentricity

20. Of the following factors leading toward the cure of the alcoholic, the MOST important is thought to be
    A. removal of all alcohol from the immediate environment
    B. development of a sense of personal adequacy
    C. social disapproval of drinking
    D. segregation from former companions
    E. intensive supervision by parole officers

21. An interview is BEST conducted in private primarily because
    A. the person interviewed will tend to be less self-conscious
    B. the interviewer will be able to maintain his continuity of thought better
    C. it will insure that the interview is *off the record*
    D. people tend to *show off* before an audience
    E. constant interruption by visitors and telephone calls will irritate the interviewer

22. An interviewer will be better able to understand the person interviewed and his problems if he recognizes that much of the person's behavior is due to motives
    A. which are deliberate
    B. of which he is unaware
    C. which are inexplicable
    D. which are kept under control
    E. which are calculated to deceive

23. When an applicant for public assistance is repeatedly told that *everything will be all right*, the effect that can usually be expected is that he will
    A. develop overt negativistic reactions toward the agency
    B. become too closely identified with the interviewer

C. doubt the interviewer's ability to understand and help with his problems
D. have greater confidence in the interviewer
E. make no appreciable change in his attitude toward the interviewer

24. While interviewing a client, it is preferable that the social service worker
    A. take no notes in order to avoid disturbing the client
    B. focus primary attention on the client while the client is talking
    C. take no notes in order to impress upon the client the worker's ability to remember all the pertinent facts of his case
    D. record all details in order to show the client that what he says is important
    E. record all details in order to impress upon the client the official character of his statements

24.____

25. During an interview, a curious applicant asks several questions about the social service worker's private life.
    As the interviewer, you should
    A. refuse to answer such questions
    B. answer his questions fully
    C. explain that your primary concern is with his problems and that discussion of your personal affairs will not be helpful in meeting his needs
    D. explain that it is the responsibility of the interviewer to ask questions and not to answer them
    E. answer only enough of his questions to the extent necessary to establish a friendly relationship with him

25.____

KEY (CORRECT ANSWERS)

1.	C	11.	C
2.	B	12.	C
3.	D	13.	D
4.	D	14.	B
5.	E	15.	E
6.	E	16.	C
7.	B	17.	E
8.	D	18.	A
9.	A	19.	E
10.	B	20.	B

21. A
22. B
23. C
24. C
25. C

TEST 5

DIRECTIONS: Each question or incomplete statement is followed by several suggested answers or completions. Select the one that BEST answers the question or completes the statement. *PRINT THE LETTER OF THE CORRECT ANSWER IN THE SPACE AT THE RIGHT.*

1. An interviewer can BEST establish a good relationship with the person being interviewed by
    A. assuming casual interest in the statements made by the person being interviewed
    B. asking questions which enable the person to show pride in his knowledge
    C. taking the point of view of the person interviewed
    D. controlling the interview to a major extent
    E. showing a genuine interest in the person

    1.____

2. An interviewer's attention must be directed toward himself as well as toward the person interviewed.
    This statement means that the interviewer should
    A. keep in mind the extent to which his own prejudices may influence his judgment
    B. rationalize the statements made by the person interviewed
    C. gain the respect and confidence of the person interviewed
    D. avoid being too impersonal
    E. avoid using indirect methods in eliciting information from the person interviewed

    2.____

3. More complete expression will be obtained from a person being interviewed if the interviewer can create the impression that
    A. the data secured will become part of a permanent record
    B. official information must be accurate in every detail
    C. it is the duty of the person interviewed to give accurate data
    D. the interviewer checks additional sources to get complete data
    E. the person interviewed is participating in a discussion of his own problems

    3.____

4. The practice of asking leading questions should be avoided in an interview because the
    A. interviewer risks revealing his attitudes to the person being interviewed
    B. interviewer may be led to ignore the objective attitudes of the person interviewed
    C. answers may be unwarrantedly influenced
    D. person interviewed will resent the attempt to lead him and will be less cooperative
    E. replies to such questions are always verbose

    4.____

5. A good technique for the interviewer to use in an effort to secure reliable data and to reduce the possibility of misunderstanding is to
   A. use casual undirected conversation, enabling the person being interviewed to talk about himself, and thus secure the desired information
   B. adopt the procedure of using direct questions regularly
   C. extract the desired information from the person being interviewed by putting him on the defensive
   D. explain to the person being interviewed the information desired and the reason for needing it
   E. explain that he is an experienced interviewer and can detect false statements

6. As a social service worker interviewing an applicant for public assistance, your attitude toward his veracity should be that the information he has furnished you is
   A. *untruthful* until you have had an opportunity to check the information
   B. *truthful* only insofar as verifiable facts are concerned
   C. *untruthful* because clients tend to interpret everything in their own favor
   D. *truthful* until you have information to the contrary
   E. *untruthful* because most applicants are unreliable

7. When a public assistance agency assigns its most experienced interviewers to conduct initial interviews with applicants, the MOST important reason for its action is that
   A. experienced workers are always older, and therefore command the respect of applicants
   B. the applicant may be given a complete understanding of the procedures to be followed and the time involved in obtaining assistance payments
   C. applicants with fraudulent intentions will be detected, and prevented from obtaining further services from the agency
   D. the agency may immediately obtain an accurate and complete plan to be followed in giving assistance to the applicant
   E. the applicant may be given an understanding of the purpose of the assistance program and of the bases for granting assistance, in addition to the routine information

8. As a social service worker conducting the first interview with an applicant for public assistance, you should
   A. ask questions requiring *yes* or *no* answers in order to simplify the interview
   B. rephrase several of the key questions as a check on his previous statements
   C. let him tell his own story while keeping him to the relevant facts
   D. avoid showing any sympathy for the applicant while he is revealing his personal needs and problems
   E. ask only direct questions so as to demonstrate your impersonal approach

9. An aged person who is unable to produce immediate proof of age has made an application for old-age assistance. He states that it will take about a week to obtain the necessary proof and that he does not have enough money to provide meals for himself until then.
   If it appears that he is in immediate need, he should be told that
   A. the law requires proof of age before any assistance can be granted
   B. temporary assistance will be provided pending the completion of the investigation
   C. a personal loan will be provided from a revolving fund
   D. he should arrange for a small loan from private sources
   E. he will have to produce an affidavit witnessed by two relatives who will vouch for the accuracy of his statements before any assistance can be provided

9.____

10. If the social service worker learns during the interview that the client has applied for public assistance without the knowledge of her husband, even though he is a member of the same household, the worker should
    A. appear not to notice this oversight, but watch for other evidences of marital discord
    B. make no mention of this to the applicant, but before taking final action send a note to the husband asking him to come in
    C. discuss this situation with the client and help her recognize the value of her husband's participation in the application
    D. point out to the applicant the implications of her behavior and ask for an explanation of her motives
    E. tell the applicant that the husband's needs will be excluded from the budget until he appears for a personal interview

10.____

11. Responsibility for fully informing the public about the availability of public assistance can MOST successfully be discharged by
    A. local public assistance agencies   B. social service exchanges
    C. community chest organizations   D. councils of social agencies
    E. service clubs

11.____

12. Of the sources through which a welfare agency can seek information about the family background and economic needs of a particular client, the MOST important consists of
    A. records and documents covering the client
    B. interviews with the client's relatives
    C. the client's own story
    D. direct contacts with former employers
    E. information offered by the client's neighbors

12.____

13. The one of the following sources of evidence which would MOST likely to give information needed to verify residence is
    A. family affidavits   B. medical and hospital bills
    C. an original birth certificate   D. rental receipts
    E. an insurance policy

13.____

14. In public assistance agencies, vital statistics are a resource used by the workers MAINLY to
    A. help establish eligibility through verification of births, deaths, and marriages
    B. help establish eligibility through verification of divorce proceedings
    C. secure proof of unemployment and eligibility for unemployment compensation
    D. secure indices of the cost of living in the larger cities
    E. discourage applications from ineligible persons

14.____

15. Case record should be considered confidential in order to
    A. make it impossible for agencies to know each other's methods
    B. permit worker to make objective rather than subjective comments
    C. prevent recipients from comparing amounts of assistance given to different families
    D. keep pertinent information from other social workers
    E. protect clients and their families

15.____

16. Because the social service worker generally is not trained as a psychiatrist, he should, when encountering psychiatric problems in the performance of his departmental duties,
    A. ignore such problems because they are beyond the scope of his responsibilities
    B. inform the affected persons that he recognizes their problems personally but will take no official cognizance of them
    C. ask to be relieved of the cases in which these problems are met and recommend that they be assigned to a psychiatrist
    D. recognize such problems where they exist and make referrals to the proper sources for treatment
    E. ask his supervisor to assign a psychiatric case worker to accompany him on all subsequent visits to the client

16.____

17. The family budget is a device used by the Department of Social Services to
    A. determine changes in the cost-of-living index
    B. estimate the needs of families and the amount of assistance necessary to meet this needs
    C. evaluate its financial condition
    D. estimate probable expenditures during a given period
    E. determine whether an applicant is eligible for categorical assistance or for general relief

17.____

18. The amount included for food for each client in Department of Social Services budgets should
    A. be based on quantitative caloric estimates of energy requirements rather than on variety in the kinds of foods
    B. be high enough to provide minimum subsistence, but low enough to discourage ineligible applicants
    C. exclude special dietary needs which are relatively expensive

18.____

D. cover food idiosyncrasies of various members of the household
E. meet the generally accepted standards for proper nutrition

19. The program for aid to dependent children is PRIMARILY directed toward
    A. the placement and supervision of children in selected foster homes
    B. provision of assistance whereby children can remain in their own homes or in the homes of relatives
    C. rehabilitation of neglected and delinquent children
    D. provision of specialized services to children in areas of special need
    E. provision of assistance to widows of good moral character for the care of their children

19.____

20. Since need is a condition of eligibility in the old-age assistance program, an assistance payment to an aged recipient should be based upon a consideration of
    A. the length of time he received general relief prior to his application for old-age assistance
    B. his attitude toward the agency
    C. his total needs and resources
    D. the probable duration of his dependency
    E. the average monthly cost of institutional care

20.____

21. From a social point of view, the reason for the growth of the practice of giving public assistance in the form of cash payments is the
    A. resultant reduction in complaints coming to the agency
    B. increased necessity for developing nationwide comparative statistics
    C. facilitation of recovery for relief improperly granted
    D. public's increasing belief in the essential justice of this type of assistance

21.____

22. In closing the case of a client, the social service worker should attempt to give the client a(n)
    A. feeling of being rejected by the agency as a worthy person
    B. idea of the progress of similar cases being handled by the agency
    C. understanding that his case could be reopened for full relief, if necessary, but not for emergency assistance
    D. explanation of the conditions upon which he might make re-application
    E. explanation of the limitations of the agency in meeting his needs

22.____

23. There is widespread agreement among nearly all planning groups concerned with public assistance that
    A. need for public assistance should be the primary, if not the only, condition of eligibility; and that all arbitrary conditions of eligibility such as citizenship, ownership of home, and moral character should be eliminated from all public assistance programs
    B. public assistance grants should be paid by voucher rather than in cash because most recipients do not use cash allowances for the purposes for which they are intended
    C. the names of persons receiving public assistance should be publicized in order to prevent fraud

23.____

D. public assistance should be discontinued immediately whenever the unemployed father of a family receiving assistance refuses a job offer
E. public assistance should not be provided for any persons who own property or who have any financial resources

24. Of fundamental importance to the work of social worker in the Department of Social Services is
    A. the knowledge of when to use the power of the Department to subdue an angry client
    B. an ability to classify clients according to common characteristics as described in case records
    C. the ability to explain eligibility in terms of legal requirements with clarity and simplicity
    D. the realization that persons who apply for public assistance have become independent because of lack of industriousness and are therefore unable to manage their own affairs
    E. a general knowledge of the executive, administrative, and supervisory functions of the Department

25. Although a social worker in the Department of Social Services has several responsibilities, his PRIMARY one is to
    A. nullify any restrictive rules and regulations issued by the State Department of Social Welfare
    B. carry out his own interpretation of the function of the Department of Social Services
    C. carry out the objectives of Department of Social Services programs as set forth in the Social Welfare Law
    D. avoid community criticism of the manner in which the programs of the Department of Social Services are conducted
    E. give relief to all applicants who claim they are eligible

KEY (CORRECT ANSWERS)

1.	E	11.	A
2.	A	12.	C
3.	E	13.	D
4.	C	14.	A
5.	D	15.	E
6.	D	16.	D
7.	E	17.	B
8.	C	18.	E
9.	B	19.	B
10.	C	20.	C

21.	D
22.	D
23.	A
24.	C
25.	C

EXAMINATION SECTION
TEST 1

DIRECTIONS: Each question or incomplete statement is followed by several suggested answers or completions. Select the one that BEST answers the question or completes the statement. *PRINT THE LETTER OF THE CORRECT ANSWER IN THE SPACE AT THE RIGHT.*

1. For children, divorce has been identified as a risk factor for 1.____
    I. being abused
    II. substance abuse
    III. lower academic achievement
    IV. criminal involvement

    A. I and II
    B. II and III
    C. II, III and IV
    D. I, II, III and IV

2. In formulating useful goals with clients, a social worker is guided by several principles. Which of the following is NOT one of these principles? 2.____

    A. Goal formulation is often delimited by the purpose of the agency, and may necessitate referral.
    B. It is necessary to designate a target person whose condition is to be changed or maintained.
    C. Goals should always be stated positively in terms of *doing* something, rather than simply *not doing* something.
    D. The establishment of a time frame for achievement is counterproductive in the formulation of goals.

3. In selecting members for group social work, homogeneity will prove most important regarding 3.____

    A. intelligence
    B. ethnicity
    C. age, especially for young children
    D. common interests

4. A practitioner will probably NOT work well with diverse populations if he 4.____

    A. believes he is free from any racist attitudes, beliefs, or feelings
    B. is comfortable with the differences between himself and clients
    C. is flexible in applying theories to specific situations
    D. is open to being challenged and teste

5. "Non-verbal" messages of practitioners and clients refer to 5.____

    A. statements that nobody should be permitted to make in an interpersonal relationship
    B. ideas and thoughts that are left unrevealed

111

C. written or otherwise documented statements about problems, recommendations, and solutions
D. the entire range of facial and body expressions that communicate feelings

6. During an assessment interview, a social worker should usually avoid asking _____ questions.

   A. "why"
   B. probing
   C. open-ended
   D. closed-ended

7. Common goals of foster parent organizations include each of the following, EXCEPT

   A. elevating the public's regard for foster care
   B. the facilitation of adoption by foster parents
   C. influencing legislation that concerns children and natural parents
   D. disseminating information among foster parents

8. "Homeostasis" is a concept that has been traditionally used to describe how

   A. organisms maintain a constant external environment,
   B. organisms keep themselves stable through self-regulating mechanisms
   C. humans tend to form groups or tribes around food supplies
   D. humans display a broad but fixed range of behaviors

9. A practitioner welcomes a client at the door of his office by saying, "Come in and sit down." He gestures to the room and the chair inside. This gesture is a _____ of the practitioner's verbal message

   A. complementation
   B. repetition
   C. regulation
   D. contradiction

10. In interviewing clients, practitioners should be careful to avoid nonverbal behaviors that are generally considered to be negative. These gestures include each of the following, EXCEPT

    A. body rotated slightly away from the client
    B. crossing and recrossing legs
    C. slightly backward body lean
    D. frequent eye contact

11. A practitioner asks himself: "Is our agency's program doing what it had hoped to do?" He is asking himself a _____ question.

    A. client outcome assessment
    B. intervention effectiveness
    C. process evaluation
    D. program evaluation

12. Of the following, which provides the BEST definition of the process of social work?

- A. A distinct set of skills that allow the worker to tap into a variety of skills to improve conditions surrounding the client system
- B. A helping activity undertaken to improve social functioning through direct involvement with the client or the systems that impact him
- C. A series of programmed interventions designed to shape the client and his environment
- D. A professional service to people in need who are unwilling or unable to act in their own best interests

13. Which of the following is NOT a basic component of social work "competence," as defined by the NASW?

    - A. Accepting responsibility or employment only on the basis of existing competence or the intention to acquire the necessary competence.
    - B. Not allowing their personal problems, psychosocial distress, legal problems, substance abuse, or mental health difficulties to interfere with professional judgment and performance.
    - C. Basing practice on recognized knowledge, including empirically based knowledge, relevant to social work and social work ethics.
    - D. Striving to become and remain proficient in professional practice and the performance of professional functions.

14. For practitioners who hope to draw upon Piaget's theory of cognitive development in their work with clients, probably the biggest shortcoming of his theory is that it

    - A. does not examine any cognitive development beyond adolescence
    - B. pigeonholes clients into distinct categories
    - C. excludes questions of morality
    - D. does not examine behavioral components of cognitions

15. Which of the following is true of institutional discrimination?

    - A. It is often concealed through legal maneuverings.
    - B. It is limited to large, formal organizations.
    - C. It is woven into the fabric of society.
    - D. It is a construction of the elite.

16. In the solution-focused model of intervention, the best way to solve problems is to

    - A. discover when the client is not having a problem, and then build on that
    - B. understand the goals and ambitions of the client
    - C. determine the function that the problematic behavior serves for the client
    - D. define the problem in terms of the client's external environment

17. A child in Piaget's preoperational stage
    - I. is capable of altruism
    - II. uses transductive reasoning
    - III. is egocentric
    - IV. derives thought from sensation and movement

    - A. I and II
    - B. I, III and IV

C. II and III
D. I, II, III and IV

18. Which of the following is NOT a primary human motive?

    A. Desire for competence
    B. Avoidance of pain
    C. Thirst
    D. Hunger

19. Summarizing clients' statements is an active listening strategy that is often useful for distilling statements into their important elements. The FIRST step in developing a good summarization of client statements during an interview is to

    A. covertly restating the message or series of messages to yourself
    B. listening for the presence of "feeling" words
    C. ask the client to summarize for herself
    D. identify any relevant patterns themes, or multiple elements

20. Each of the following is considered to be a desirable outcome of an initial interview with an applicant for social services, EXCEPT that the applicant

    A. leaves confident of working with the practitioner or case manager toward a satisfactory solution
    B. understands his/her responsibilities in the treatment or intervention
    C. feels free to express him/herself
    D. feeling some rapport with the practitioner or case manager

21. When counseling clients, social work practitioners will generally be effective if they
    I. are able to recognize and accept their own power
    II. can focus on the present moment
    III. remain in the active process of developing their own counseling style
    IV. are not afraid to offer advice

    A. I and III
    B. I, II and III
    C. II, III and IV
    D. I, II, III and IV

22. According to the NASW's code of ethics, social workers who have direct knowledge of a social work colleague's incompetence should FIRST

    A. consult with that colleague when feasible and assist the colleague in taking remedial action
    B. take action through the appropriate channels established by the employers or agency
    C. notify the NASW and any appropriate licensing and regulating bodies
    D. solicit the opinion of at least one other social worker with approximately equal qualifications and responsibilities to determine a course of action

23. Countertransference, if recognized by the practitioner, can be a useful element in a client relationship. Often, however, it is not helpful or even hurtful. Hurtful forms typically involve each of the following, EXCEPT countertransference that

A. causes a practitioner to emit subtle clues that "lead" the client
B. causes a practitioner to adopt the role the client wants us to play in his or her traditional "script"
C. is used at a distance to generate empathy for the client
D. blinds a practitioner from an important area of exploration

24. During any intervention, a social worker's final activities are aimed at _____ in the client's everyday functioning.
    I. stabilizing success
    II. generalizing outcomes
    III. preventing recidivism
    IV. restricting options

    A. I and II
    B. I and III
    C. II, III and IV
    D. I, II, III and IV

25. In the documentation and report writing phase of assessment, a service coordinator's documentation responsibilities usually consist of

    A. social histories and intake summaries
    B. medical and social histories
    C. staff notes and mental status examinations
    D. intake summaries and staff notes

26. A social work practitioner is MOST likely to increase the chances of his clients' connecting with the appropriate services when he

    A. refers clients to other more skilled professionals in the hope that these professionals will be able to determine how best to meet the clients' needs
    B. promotes self determination by providing a list of agencies in the area and allowing the clients to decide who can best meet their needs
    C. acquire expertise in as many areas of social work practice as possible, in order to directly provide needed services
    D. becomes knowledgeable about programs and providers available, and actively brokers needed services

27. One explanation for the steady increase in the divorce rate in the United States is that industrialization and urbanization led to a change in the roles played by family members. This explanation is consistent with the _____ perspective.

    A. symbolic interaction
    B. structural functionalist
    C. subcultural
    D. social conflict

28. One of the most significant criticisms about the use of strategic planning in human services organizations is that it

    A. leaves many stakeholders in the dark about the organization's objectives
    B. limits responsiveness to changing community needs

C. erodes employee morale and commitment to the organizational mission
D. is often too abstract to be useful in day-to-day management

29. The way in which a practitioner conceptualizes a client's problem configuration is known as

    A. conceptualization
    B. the internal working model
    C. mental set
    D. framing

30. Significant factors that have contributed to the changing nature of American families since the 1970s include
    I. an increase in births outside marriage
    II. a greater number of remarriages in which partners bring children from previous relationships
    III. altered gender role expectations
    IV. an increase in the number of partners who divorce or separate

    A. I, II and IV
    B. I and III
    C. III only
    D. I, II, III and IV

31. Culture maintains boundaries in each of the following ways, EXCEPT by

    A. instilling a sense of genuineness about the alternatives peculiar to a society
    B. constructing symbols and meanings
    C. limiting the ranges of acceptable behavior and attitudes
    D. establishing the tendency for people to think of other societies as inferior

32. The solution-focused perspective defines a client who describes a problem but isn't willing to work on solving it as a

    A. resistor
    B. complainant
    C. dam-builder
    D. procrastinator

33. During an assessment interview, a practitioner is trying to identify the range of problems that a client is experiencing. Which of the following communication skills is most appropriately used for this purpose?

    A. Open-ended questions
    B. Closed-ended questions
    C. Confrontation
    D. Interpretation

34. Social workers who have unresolved personal conflicts should

    A. recognize that their problems may interfere with the effectiveness and avoid activities or responses that could harm a client
    B. repress any anxiety-provoking issues in their own lives before attempting to work with others

C. use their experience to lead clients in a mutual resolution of these problems
D. resolve these conflicts before planning a client intervention and ideally, before meeting the client at all.

35. Based largely on the understanding that all people break rules at one time or another, _____ theorists make the assumption that what we call "deviant" is actually part of an overall pattern of normality.

    A. labeling
    B. social Darwinism
    C. conflict
    D. order

36. Rural clients tend to evaluate social workers on the basis of

    A. the level of education the worker has achieved
    B. help delivered or problems solved
    C. the type of intervention used
    D. areas of specialization

37. A client is having trouble at work. He tells the practitioner "I have a hard time relating to authority figures." He is describing his problem behavior

    A. in a way that places responsibility squarely on himself
    B. covertly
    C. in nonbehavioral terms
    D. without any affective cues

38. The practice of limiting a client's right to self-determination in order to protect him or her from self-harm is known in social work as

    A. gatekeeping
    B. paternalism
    C. delimiting behavior
    D. proxy

39. Which of the following is LEAST likely to be a symptom of stress?

    A. Emotional instability
    B. Lethargy
    C. Sleep problems
    D. Digestive problems

40. In the traditional clinical model of school social work, a practitioner was probably LEAST likely to execute the role of

    A. enabler
    B. consultant
    C. supporter
    D. advocate

41. When advocating for a client, the first attempt at advocacy should always be

    A. a legal challenge
    B. a formal appeal
    C. temperate persuasion
    D. widely spread publicity about the client's case

42. During regular meetings with his practitioner, a client has the tendency to ascribe the achievements of others to good luck or easy tasks, while assuming his failures to be due to a lack of ability or experience. The client's thinking is a phenomenon known as

    A. fundamental attribution bias
    B. the Hawthorne effect
    C. self-serving bias
    D. the halo effect

43. The responsibilities of social work intern instructors typically include each of the following, EXCEPT

    A. clearly stating roles and responsibilities of interns in the field
    B. clearly stating the roles and responsibilities of site supervisors
    C. acting on site supervisors' recommendations following a negative intern evaluation
    D. developing clear field placement policies

44. A teenage client has been having problems in school he is constantly being disciplined for being disruptive. Discussions with the client reveal that even though he has lost several privileges at school, he is reluctant to give up his disruptive behavior because of the attention it brings in from his peers. The attention of the client's peers is an example of a(n)

    A. secondary gain
    B. behavioral consequence
    C. negative reinforcement
    D. cognitive dissonance

45. Which of the following is NOT a typical purpose of client self-monitoring?

    A. To shift the burden of decision-making onto the client
    B. To validate the accuracy of the client's reports during interviews
    C. To test out hunches about the problem.
    D. To help practitioner and client gain information about what actually occurs with respect to the problem in real-life situations

46. Which of the following is a "lower-order" human need, as identified in Maslow's hierarchy?

    A. Belonging
    B. Status
    C. Fulfillment
    D. Security

47. Gene, a social worker, finds himself wanting to solve his client's problems with alcohol dependency, which are similar to problems Gene's own son went through several years ago. Gene gives advice and is frustrated when the client doesn't follow through on his suggestions. Gene's emotional reactions to his client are based on

   A. countertransference
   B. nurturing
   C. transference
   D. empathy

48. In the termination phase of treatment, strategies for maintaining client gains may include each of the following, EXCEPT

   A. increasing the client's sense of mastery through realistic praise
   B. anticipating and planning for possible future difficulties
   C. highlighting and specifying the client's role in maintaining change
   D. teaching the client to deal with problems that underlie a coping pattern

49. After receiving a notification about a 10-year-old boy's underperfor-mance at school, a social worker has tried twice to arrange a meeting with the boy's 28-year-old mother, who works long hours as a waitress and has sole responsibility for his care. Both times, the mother has cancelled the meeting at the last minute, citing sudden work conflicts.
The social worker schedules an in-home visit to the boy's familybut when he arrives, he is told by the boy that the mother is at work. The child's grandmother also lives in the home, but is bedridden, and the boy and his sister help care for her. The family's apartment is in disarray, with dirty dishes stacked in the sink and on the stovetop. Laundry is strewn about in wrinkled piles. The social worker observes no alcohol in the house, and the grandmother, who is cooperative, says that her daughter doesn't drink, and never has.
As the social worker continues to monitor this family, he should be especially alert for signs of

   A. a personality disorder on the part of the mother
   B. child abuse
   C. substance abuse
   D. child neglect

50. Within practice settings that call upon the practitioner's knowledge and skill at all levels of the organization, the social work profession is considered to be a(n) _____ discipline.

   A. primary
   B. secondary
   C. collegial
   D. ancillary

51. Among gays and lesbians, stress and a lack of emotional support have been shown to contribute to

   A. high rates of alcoholism
   B. promiscuity
   C. identity fragmentation
   D. erratic employment patterns

52. An elderly client is particularly concerned about being "bothered" all the time by a social work practitioner who frequently visits her home. To avoid too much discomfort on the part of the client, the practitioner has the client sign several blank consent forms so that her medical history can be sent to several agencies that might offer supportive services. In this case, the worker has

   A. violated the principle of informed consent
   B. hit upon a key strategy for avoiding burnout
   C. demonstrated ignorance of the eligibility rules for most service agencies
   D. found an ethical strategy for streamlining an often frustrating bureaucracy

53. The most common diagnoses for people who complete suicide are

   A. schizophrenia and substance abuse
   B. depressive illness and borderline personality disorder
   C. depressive illness and alcoholism
   D. schizophrenia and chronic metabolic disease

54. The mother of a 14-year-old girl telephoned crisis services, telling the worker that her son had just locked and barricaded himself in his room. Earlier, she had overheard a conversation between the boy and his girlfriend that was clearly a fight. She is concerned because the boy had tried to overdose after the end of an earlier relationship.
   A worker was immediately dispatched to the residence. After a lengthy conversation in which the worker successfully established rapport with the boy, the boy agreed to let the worker in.
   Thus far, crisis services and the worker have followed the formula of Roberts' Seven-Stage Crisis Intervention Model. As a next step, the worker will attempt to

   A. explore alternatives to suicide, such as inpatient or outpatient services
   B. identify and validate the boy's emotions
   C. develop an action plan with the boy
   D. have the boy identify what he views as the major problem or problems

55. The primary goal of crisis intervention can best be described as

   A. protecting the client from a situation in which he or she has become more likely to experience a traumatic event than other people
   B. helping the client to identify and endure the long-term consequences of a traumatic event
   C. protecting a client from self-harm following a traumatic event
   D. helping the client to identify and cope with the sense of "disequilibrium" in the aftermath of a trauma

56. A practitioner discovers that a client is behaving in a way that is seriously damaging both to himself and a close relative. While respecting the concept of self-determination and confidentiality, the practitioner should

   A. warn the client that he (the practitioner) has an obligation to divulge the client's behavior to the appropriate agency or authority, and then do so
   B. attempt to dissuade the client from further engaging in behavior that is harmful
   C. immediately alert the authorities
   D. refer the client to a social services worker who has more experience in this specific type of behavior

57. In order to serve effectively in rural communities, social work practitioners would most likely need to incorporate the concepts of _____ into their practice.

    A. nature and seasonal fluctuation
    B. self-reliance and mutual aid
    C. land and ownership
    D. religion and spirituality

58. Which of the following is NOT typically included in a service agreement between a practitioner and a client?

    A. Description of the agency's programs and services
    B. Fees for service or arrangements for reimbursement
    C. Theoretical framework for the relationship
    D. Time frames for the provision of services

59. From a legal perspective, case records

    A. belong to the practitioner who created them
    B. belong to the client
    C. belong to the agency at which they are physically held
    D. are for the benefit of the client

60. A practitioner is speaking to a client via cellular phone. The practitioner should be aware that
    I. there is a chance that the call could be intercepted by an unauthorized party
    II. the client may not be in a private place
    III. telephone conversations are not considered to be a public service
    IV. complete privacy cannot be assured

    A. I and II
    B. I, II, and IV
    C. III only
    D. I, II, III and IV

61. The basic assumptions underlying social work administration do NOT include the statement that

    A. each person who works within the agency should be considered a stakeholder in agency outcomes
    B. administration is largely the process of securing and transforming community resources
    C. the major contributions toward the improvement of administration come from management itself
    D. the agency has the primary responsibility for the creation and control of its own destiny

62. Most Asian Americans who are seeking from a social work practitioner are looking for a professional who is

    A. nondirective
    B. problem-focused
    C. goal-oriented
    D. experiential in focus

63. Privileged communication is NOT

   A. widely varying in state-to-state legal definitions
   B. usually waived if a third party is present
   C. particularly difficult to protect when working with married couples
   D. protected no matter what the risks involved

64. In devising a treatment plan, a practitioner begins with client tasks that can be managed fairly easily and with some success, before moving on to the larger issues that are causing problems. In doing so, the practitioner is adhering to the rule of

   A. successive approximations
   B. object orientation
   C. positive reinforcement
   D. mental set

65. "Preparatory empathy" is a process that is used by a practitioner in order to

   A. insure against client deception
   B. streamline an intervention by figuring some things out in advance
   C. choose necessary resources or services
   D. make him more aware of issues or barriers that might be encountered

66. The federal WIC program specifically targets the health and welfare of

   A. abused children
   B. adoptive families
   C. pregnant women and newborn children
   D. unskilled laborers who have been injured on the job

67. Of all Hispanics living the United States, those of Mexican descent account for about _____ percent of the total.

   A. 20
   B. 40
   C. 60
   D. 80

68. From her first few meetings with a client, a social work practitioner has begun to form an impression. If the practitioner seeks out additional information that will help to confirm or deny her existing impressions, she will be engaging in

   A. cognitive integration
   B. active perception
   C. offensive perception
   D. thematic apperception

69. A social worker is using the person-in-environment (PIE) system of client assessment. In describing the environmental problems that affect a client's social functioning, the social worker will rely on six groupings of social system problems. Which of the following is NOT one of the groupings used in the PIE system?

   A. Economic/basic need
   B. Judicial/legal system

C. Physical health
D. Education and training

70. Basic social work values that influence professional practice include each of the following, EXCEPT 70.____

   A. self-determination
   B. the inherent uniqueness of a person
   C. individualism
   D. the inherent worth and dignity of a person

71. Which step in the listening process involves the assignment of meaning to a message? 71.____

   A. Encoding
   B. Attending
   C. Understanding
   D. Selecting

72. Qualitative social work research 72.____

   A. observes people in natural settings and focuses on the meaning they assign to experiences.
   B. is analyzed through the use of bivariate methods
   C. details the past in order to understand present conditions
   D. compares statistics from number of cases

73. When a worker attempts to "cement" a referral, she is attempting to 73.____

   A. make sure the client is connected to the suggested resource
   B. make the working relationship into a strong enough bond that the client will be sure to follow through
   C. use software or another evaluative tool that confirms the appropriateness of the client to the proposed resource
   D. suggest to the client in advance that the referral will result in success

74. In working with a client, a practitioner is careful to avoid singling out one or two obvious client characteristics as the reason for everything the person does. The tendency to do this is known as 74.____

   A. stereotyping
   B. scripting
   C. over-attribution
   D. highballing

75. A group's sense of ethnic identity is affected by the
    I. degree to which the members' physical appearances differ from those in mainstream society
    II. size of the group
    III. amount of power the group has
    IV. extent of assimilation

    A. I only
    B. I and III
    C. II and IV
    D. I, II, III and IV

KEY (CORRECT ANSWERS)

1. D	16. A	31. A	46. D	61. C
2. D	17. C	32. B	47. A	62. A
3. C	18. A	33. A	48. D	63. D
4. A	19. A	34. A	49. D	64. A
5. D	20. B	35. A	50. A	65. D
6. A	21. B	36. B	51. A	66. C
7. B	22. A	37. C	52. A	67. C
8. B	23. C	38. B	53. C	68. B
9. B	24. A	39. B	54. D	69. C
10. D	25. D	40. D	55. D	70. C
11. D	26. D	41. C	56. A	71. C
12. B	27. B	42. A	57. B	72. A
13. A	28. D	43. C	58. C	73. A
14. A	29. A	44. A	59. B	74. C
15. C	30. D	45. A	60. B	75. D

TEST 2

DIRECTIONS: Each question or incomplete statement is followed by several suggested answers or completions. Select the one that BEST answers the question or completes the statement. *PRINT THE LETTER OF THE CORRECT ANSWER IN THE SPACE AT THE RIGHT.*

1. In the _____ style of conflict management, the parties attempt to separate themselves from the problem.

    A. cooperative
    B. nonconfrontational
    C. mediative
    D. settlement

    1.____

2. The purposes of staff notes, or progress notes, include
    I. recording client's responses to services
    II. connecting a service to a key issue
    III. describing client status
    IV. providing direction for ongoing treatment

    A. I only
    B. I, II and III
    C. III and IV
    D. I, II, III and IV

    2.____

3. A genogram is an assessment tool that

    A. involves DNA sampling
    B. defers consideration of current family relationships
    C. gives a picture of family relationships over at least three generations
    D. uses statistical measures to calculate the probability of an intervention's success

    3.____

4. Which of the following is NOT a belief of stage theorists?

    A. The progression of stages is biologically programmed.
    B. Children pass through the same stages in the same sequence.
    C. Stages are usually marked by age ranges.
    D. As children progress through the stages, the differences between them are quantitative.

    4.____

5. During the opening phase of a client interview, the practitioner should probably spend most of his time and thoughts on

    A. self-disclosure
    B. negotiating a working contract
    C. interpreting behaviors
    D. explaining agency rules and protocols

    5.____

6. Behaviors commonly associated with substance abuse include
    I. a withdrawal from responsibility
    II. unusual outbreaks of temper
    III. abrupt changes in quality or output of work
    IV. wearing sunglasses at inappropriate times

    6.____

A. I and II
B. I, II and III
C. II and IV
D. I, II, III and IV

7. Which of the following would a practitioner typically do FIRST in a problem assessment interview?

    A. Identify client coping skills
    B. Identify the range of client problems
    C. Prioritize and select issues and problems for discussion
    D. Identify consequences of problem behaviors

8. A social worker's primary ethical duty is to

    A. effect social justice
    B. promote the welfare of the client
    C. respect diversity
    D. avoid dependent relationships

9. The person-centered model of human behavior views the major reason for maladjustment as a(n)

    A. failure to set a self-actualizing tendency in motion
    B. inability to establish unconditional positive regard
    C. incongruence between self-concept and experience
    D. unresolved childhood frustrations

10. The person-in-environment (PIE) system of client assessment is a four-factor system. Factor _____ provides a statement of the client's physical health problems.

    A. I
    B. II
    C. III
    D. IV

11. An adolescent client tells her social worker that she feels she is the only person in the world who has ever had such strong unrequited love for another person—the boy who sits next to her in geometry class. The component of adolescent egocentrism being enacted by the girl is the

    A. all-or-none fallacy
    B. imaginary audience
    C. questionable cause
    D. personal fable

12. Research into interpersonal relationships suggests that women often build relationships through shared positive feelings, while men often build relationships through

    A. shared activities
    B. shared opinions
    C. metacommunication
    D. impression management

13. Which of the following is NOT typically a purpose of assessment? 13.____

    A. To identify the controlling or contributing variables associated with a client's problem
    B. To launch the first phase of treatment
    C. To educate and motivate the client by sharing views about the problem
    D. To plan effective interventions and strategies

14. Persuading clients to abandon mistaken ways of thinking is a goal of 14.____

    A. client-centered therapy
    B. operant conditioning
    C. cognitive therapy
    D. systematic desensitization

15. A practitioner is creating an action plan with an adult client who has decided to leave his current job. Typically, planning such a move requires practitioner and client to move on to 15.____

    A. ensure that the work to be done fits an accepted model of treatment
    B. breaking large goals into component parts
    C. making the client aware of the full range of consequences
    D. ensure that this decision meets with the approval of the people who will be affected by it

16. Some of the information in an applicant's file comes from secondary sources. Which of the following is NOT considered a secondary source? 16.____

    A. Applicant's family
    B. Referring agency
    C. School
    D. Current staff notes

17. Self-disclosure is considered a "discretionary" response in discussions with clients, because it 17.____

    A. is not considered to be therapeutic
    B. is only used if the client requests it
    C. should be used carefully to avoid taking the focus off the client
    D. requires a familiarity with the client's worldview before it is used

18. For a practitioner working from the family systems theory, symptoms of maladjustment in families are usually masked by 18.____

    A. the involvement and recommendations of professionals who were previously involved
    B. the presenting crisis or problem that initially brought the family into contact with the agency
    C. abusive relationships
    D. environmental components in the family's community

19. A school social worker is told that one of the kindergartners is running around, out of control, and disrupting the others at naptime. As she attempts to understand the problem, her FIRST step should be to 19.____

A. arrange an interview with the school psychologist
B. look into finding an alternative school placement
C. systematically observe the child in the classroom to see how it is managed
D. contact the parents to inform them of the child's behavior problems

20. What is the collective term applied to communication variables such as voice level, pitch, rate, and fluency of speech?

    A. Kinesics
    B. Paralinguistics
    C. Nonverbal messages
    D. Proxemics

21. Although the terms *counseling* and *interviewing* are sometimes used interchangeably in social work, there are differences that should be noted. Which of the following is NOT one of these differences.

    A. Interviewing is a responsibility that can be assumed by most practitioners or case managers.
    B. Interviewing is a more basic process for information gathering and problem solving.
    C. Counseling is a more intensive and personal process.
    D. Counseling is often associated with nonprofessional workers, whereas therapy used to indicate professional interventions.

22. A social worker in the _____ role is conducting "macro" practice.
    I. manager
    II. planner
    III. case manager
    IV. mediator

    A. I and II
    B. I, II and IV
    C. III only
    D. I, II, III and IV

23. The final stage of Elisabeth Kubler-Ross's theory of how people handle the knowledge of their impending death is known as

    A. denial
    B. bargaining
    C. anger
    D. acceptance

24. Probably the most important factor in establishing a working alliance with a client is the

    A. client's belief about whether the practitioner attends and understands
    B. accuracy of the practitioner's assessment of the presenting problem(s)
    C. practitioner's effort to be empathetic
    D. client's initial willingness to change

25. During the assessment phase, the practice of _____ means that the practitioner and client are setting specific objectives.

    A. activating resources
    B. framing solutions
    C. defining the problem
    D. weighing alternatives

26. Reflecting and paraphrasing are two active listening strategies often used by practitioners to help clients become more aware of the implications of their own statements. Basically the difference between reflecting and paraphrasing involves the difference between the

    A. client's words and the client's actions
    B. the emotional (affective) and factual (cognitive) content of messages
    C. way the client perceives the world and the way the world actually is
    D. way the client is expressing a message and the way it is being received by the practitioner

27. The process by which people shape social life by adapting to, negotiating with, and changing social structures is known as

    A. determinism
    B. positivism
    C. human agency
    D. ideology

28. Child welfare is a social work practice area that

    A. focuses on issues, problems, and policies related to the well-being of children
    B. administers school lunches and other benefit programs for low-income children
    C. focuses on increasing the educational potential of children
    D. mainly works to broker adoptions

29. The relationship between social work supervisors and supervisees, which parallels the relationship between social worker and client, has been described in terms of basic relational elements. Which of the following is NOT one of these?

    A. Caring
    B. Rapport
    C. Authority
    D. Trust

30. The _____ model attributes the essential characteristics of consensus, cohesion, stability, reciprocity, and cooperation to society.

    A. evolutionary
    B. conflict
    C. order
    D. symbolic interaction

31. Upholding rules, regulations and restrictions of a social services agency which are not always best for the client is a function of the social worker's role known as

    A. gatekeeping
    B. spoilage
    C. advocacy
    D. bureaucratic blindness

32. A social worker and her client have developed a long-range goal. Now they are determining individual steps that will lead to the achievement of that goal. This is a process known as

    A. chunking
    B. prioritizing
    C. partializing
    D. contracting

33. Community surveys, policy analyses, and case histories are examples of

    A. social studies
    B. ecomaps
    C. needs assessments
    D. genograms

34. In a social services agency that serves teenage runaways, an example of a direct service strategy would be

    A. organizing
    B. counseling
    C. gathering information
    D. planning

35. Compared to others in society, those with superior _____ are more likely to support the status quo.

    A. educational achievement
    B. social locations
    C. value systems
    D. incomes

36. "Primary prevention" means

    A. the severity and duration of a disease or disorder have been reduced
    B. clinical means have been used to provide treatment, such as crisis intervention
    C. a disease or disorder is stopped at its source, and the cause is eliminated
    D. the spread of a disease or disorder among people has been limited

37. Under normal circumstances it is considered acceptable practice for a social worker to disclose a client's confidential information to

    I. the practitioner's supervisor as it relates to the supervisory relationship
    II. professionals who are consulted about assessments or interventions
    III. third-party payers for the purpose of justifying treatment decisions
    IV. close family members for the purpose of developing understanding of the client's particular difficulties

A. I only
B. I and II
C. I, II and III
D. I, II, III and IV

38. A client's feelings of powerlessness can be reduced when a social worker adopts each of the following roles, EXCEPT the role of

    A. resource consultant, who connects the client to goods and services
    B. advocate, who acts as the client's protector in social living matters
    C. sensitizer, who helps the client gain knowledge needed to solve problems
    D. educator, who facilitates the learning and skill development needed for goal setting and task completion

39. The _____ model of human services organization management places the greatest value on maximizing the productivity of the organization.

    A. internal process
    B. open-system
    C. rational goal
    D. human relations

40. During an interview, practitioner and client establish a goal for the client to use her time more efficiently at work and at home. This is an example of a _____ goal.

    A. process
    B. survival
    C. treatment
    D. service

41. One reason people often confuse race and ethnicity is because they

    A. are suspicious of people who are different from themselves
    B. are unaware that race is cultural and ethnicity is biological
    C. see cultural differences and define race in specific, often inaccurate ways
    D. have met few people outside their own race

42. Dual relationships between a practitioner and a client, according to the NASW:

    A. should not be formed if there is any possibility for exploitation or potential harm to the client
    B. are usually an unavoidable part of professional practice
    C. are generally acceptable if social workers take steps to protect clients
    D. are generally acceptable if social workers are careful to avoid legal problems that could damage the status of the social work profession

43. In a family intervention that implements the structural model, the family will be expected to

    A. submit to the direction of the practitioner
    B. solve their own problems
    C. shift their internal alliances
    D. shift blame to the external environment

44. In diversion programs, social workers typically provide

   A. case management services with probation officers in an attempt to prevent recidivism
   B. consultation services about early-release programs for juvenile offenders
   C. counseling services through a network of lay professionals
   D. crisis intervention or referral services aimed at avoiding imprisonment

45. In hospital social work, an example of macropractice would be

   A. connecting with community providers to maintain understanding of community needs
   B. increasing health provider awareness of clients' home environment
   C. engaging clients in planning for their immediate future after discharge
   D. educating clients and families about the implications of a particular illness or disorder

46. A client tells a practitioner that he is distraught over the end of his marriage and wishes he could "just go to sleep forever, be at peace, and not have to feel this pain any more." The practitioner should

   A. assess whether the client is suicidal and intervene if necessary
   B. recognize that such statements are often merely a "cry for help" and urge the client to focus on more practical issues
   C. contact the client's wife and determine whether there is a chance to reconcile
   D. immediately commit the client to a psychiatric facility

47. The presenting problems of most African American clients are rooted in

   A. genetics
   B. personality deficits
   C. stress from external systems
   D. unresolved family conflicts

48. A solution-focused intervention would most likely involve the goal of

   A. a first-order change in the client system
   B. behavioral continuity
   C. a perceptual shift from talking about problems to talking about how to solve them
   D. determining exactly how a problem came into being

49. During an interview in which a client is being evaluated, the client should understand that the

   A. information gained during the interview may be the basis of a report on the client
   B. questions will not be upsetting to him/her
   C. interview will focus on the client's well-being
   D. he or she has implicitly entered into a service contract

50. The _____ theory of rural social work asserts that there are distinct differences between rural and urban areas, and that the urban end of the continuum is associated with social pathology.

A. classical
B. subcultural
C. compositional
D. determinist

51. During the supervisory discussion of a client case, the FIRST topic of discussion should typically be

A. client dynamics and problems
B. alternative intervention strategies
C. a tentative assessment or diagnosis
D. selection of a general treatment approach

51._____

52. The millions of Asian Americans living in the United States today represent a generally _____ population.

A. prosperous
B. culturally homogeneous
C. mainstreamed
D. heterogeneous

52._____

53. Most legal issues encountered by social work practitioners involve

A. complaints of improper conduct
B. being sued for negligence or malpractice
C. being prosecuted for crimes
D. acting as witnesses in litigation

53._____

54. The initial recommended response to a client who is suicidal is

A. hospitalization and observation
B. identifying the client's level of seriousness
C. problem-solving training
D. crisis intervention and a functional assessment of the suicidal behavior

54._____

55. The most common client reactions to the termination of direct social service include each of the following, EXCEPT

A. pride
B. ambivalence
C. satisfaction
D. denial

55._____

56. Most referrals to human service professionals are made by

A. school systems
B. health care workers
C. the courts
D. word of mouth from friends or family members

56._____

57. The term "handicap" refers to a(n)

A. obstruction that prevents an interface between a disability and the environment
B. an impairment that limits one's daily activities

57._____

C. inability to perform tasks at a level that is generally considered to be socially acceptable
D. loss of use or function of an organ or bodily system

58. When writing case notes, practitioners should always
    I. keep in mind that others may read the notes
    II. compose them immediately after a client meeting
    III. provide as much detail as possible
    IV. use shorthand

    A. I and II
    B. II only
    C. I, II and III
    D. I, II, III and

58.____

59. The most frequent cause of child death is

    A. physical abuse
    B. suicide
    C. being left unsupervised or alone for long periods of time
    D. automobile accidents

59.____

60. Clients of social service agencies often disagree with either agency policies or a practitioner's actions, or both. If a client demands to know why a particular action was taken and perhaps reverse it, he or she is exercising a right to

    A. confidentiality
    B. due process
    C. privileged information
    D. informed consent

60.____

61. Content theories of human motivation argue that

    A. most people dislike change
    B. external consequences determine behavior
    C. most people are affiliation-oriented
    D. internal needs lead to behavior

61.____

62. Once a client's service needs are clear, a social worker often helps the client choose the most appropriate service and negotiates the terms of service delivery. Here, the social worker is acting in the role of

    A. broker
    B. consultant
    C. advocate
    D. coordinator

62.____

63. When social work practitioners commit errors in working with gay, lesbian, and bisexual clients, these errors most often stem from the

    A. workers' own unconscious prejudices
    B. failure to recognize clients as homosexual, due to a lack of identifying characteristics
    C. identification of client problems as being caused by their sexuality

63.____

D. assumption that client problems are unrelated to social oppression or stigma

64. If included statistically as a form of elder abuse, self-neglect would represent about _____ percent of cases reported to state adult protective services agencies.

    A. 5-10
    B. 20-35
    C. 40-50
    D. 60-75

65. Many social workers, especially those who work in institutional settings, use the brief treatment model in their interventions. Which of the following is NOT one of the core assumptions of this model?

    A. Problems are a normal part of life and not a sign of pathology.
    B. Practitioners believe people can change, and communicate this to their clients.
    C. The purpose of treatment is to develop insight into the underlying causes of problems.
    D. Treatment makes use of what the client brings to it

66. Stan, a Native American college student, is seeking information about work programs in the urban community where he lives. When Stan asks a female practitioner at the local agency about it, the practitioner notices that he makes very little eye contact. The practitioner should recognize that Stan

    A. would be more likely to look into her eyes if she were a male
    B. is not likely to follow through with the practitioner's recommendations or referrals
    C. is likely to view direct eye contact as a lack of respect
    D. does not express much faith in the practitioner's abilities

67. The tendency of people to perceive what they expect to perceive is a phenomenon known as

    A. self-serving bias
    B. perceptual set
    C. filtration
    D. fundamental attribution bias

68. A person's satisfaction with communication is based upon a theoretical "sum total" of the positive and negative elements in a message. This sum is a phenomenon known as message

    A. validity
    B. salience
    C. solidity
    D. valence

69. Data about how long or how often a problem occurs before an intervention are known as _____ data.

    A. raw
    B. norming
    C. baseline
    D. skewed

70. In _____ social work, assessment is also known as functional analysis.

    A. narrative
    B. behavioral
    C. feminist
    D. cognitive

71. During an assessment interview, a practitioner asks a client: "How do you feel about the fact that your drinking has harmed your relationship with your daughter?" The practitioner is trying to identify _____ consequences of the client's problem.

    A. contextual
    B. affective
    C. behavioral
    D. somatic

72. For social work research to have a meaningful function, it must be applied by practitioners. One of the major reasons practitioners fail to apply the results of research is that

    A. there is no standard methodology that would make results universally applicable
    B. many studies lack relevance to day-to-day practice decisions
    C. there is still widespread theoretical bias in the design of many studies
    D. most practitioners don't conduct research themselves

73. Of the following social sciences, social work draws most of its professional expertise from

    A. psychology
    B. economics
    C. sociology
    D. anthropology

74. In her meetings with a client, a practitioner has begun to form the perception that he may be using a combination of alcohol and illegal drugs. She decides, during subsequent meetings, to engage in "direct perception checking" in order to confirm or deny this perception. This will involve

    A. paying careful attention to the client's tone of voice
    B. observing the client's behaviors to discover cues that will either confirm or deny her impressions
    C. asking the client if he has a drug or drinking problem
    D. listening more intently to the client's words and language

75. Though practitioner self-disclosure can be a useful tool for helping clients, it is most helpful when its use is carefully assessed beforehand. Generally, practitioners should AVOID making self-disclosure statements

    A. as concise as possible
    B. as a way of introducing oneself to the client
    C. in a way that will regulate the role distance between practitioner and client
    D. similar in content and mood to the client's messages

KEY (CORRECT ANSWERS)

1. A	16. D	31. A	46. A	61. D
2. D	17. C	32. C	47. C	62. A
3. C	18. B	33. A	48. C	63. B
4. D	19. C	34. B	49. A	64. C
5. B	20. B	35. B	50. A	65. C
6. D	21. D	36. C	51. A	66. C
7. C	22. A	37. B	52. D	67. B
8. B	23. D	38. B	53. D	68. D
9. C	24. A	39. C	54. D	69. C
10. D	25. B	40. C	55. D	70. B
11. D	26. B	41. C	56. D	71. B
12. A	27. C	42. A	57. A	72. B
13. B	28. A	43. B	58. C	73. A
14. C	29. C	44. D	59. C	74. B
15. B	30. C	45. A	60. B	75. B

INTERVIEWING

EXAMINATION SECTION

TEST 1

DIRECTIONS: Each question or incomplete statement is followed by several suggested answers or completions. Select the one that BEST answers the question or completes the statement. *PRINT THE LETTER OF THE CORRECT ANSWER IN THE SPACE AT THE RIGHT.*

1. Of the following, the MAIN advantage to the supervisor of using the indirect (or nondirective) interview, in which he asks only guiding questions and encourages the employee to do most of the talking, is that he can
   A. obtain a mass of information about the employee in a very short period of time
   B. easily get at facts which the employee wishes to conceal
   C. get answers which are not slanted or biased in order to win his favor
   D. effectively deal with an employee's serious emotional problems

    1.____

2. An interviewer under your supervision routinely closes his interview with a reassuring remark such as, "I'm sure you soon will be well," or "Everything will soon be all right."
   This practice is USUALLY considered
   A. *advisable*, chiefly because the interviewer may make the patient feel better
   B. *inadvisable*, chiefly because it may cause a patient who is seriously ill to doubt the worker's understanding of the situation
   C. *advisable*, chiefly because the patient becomes more receptive if further interviews are needed
   D. *inadvisable*, chiefly because the interviewer should usually not show that he is emotionally involved

    2.____

3. An interviewer has just ushered out a client he has interviewed. As the interviewer is preparing to leave, the client mentions a fact that seems to contradict the information he has given.
   Of the following, it would be BEST for the interviewer at this time to
   A. make no response but write the fact down in his report and plan to come back another day
   B. point out to the client that he has contradicted himself and ask for an explanation
   C. ask the client to elaborate on the comment and attempt to find out further information about the fact
   D. disregard the comment since the client was probably exhausted and not thinking clearly

    3.____

4. A client who is being interviewed insists on certain facts. The interviewer knows that these statements are incorrect.
In regard to the rest of the client's statements, the interviewer is MOST justified to
   A. disregard any information the client gives which cannot be verified
   B. try to discover other misstatements by confronting the client with the discrepancy
   C. consider everything else which the client has said as the truth unless proved otherwise
   D. ask the client to prove his statements

5. Immediately after the interviewer identifies himself to a client, she says in a hysterical voice that he is not to be trusted.
Of the following, the BEST course of action for the interviewer to follow would be to
   A. tell the woman sternly that if she does not stay calm, he will leave
   B. assure the woman that there is no cause to worry
   C. ignore the woman until she becomes quiet
   D. ask the woman to explain her problem

6. Assume that you are an interviewer and that one of your interviewees has asked you for advice on dealing with a personal problem.
Of the following, the BEST action for you to take is to
   A. tell him about a similar problem which you know worked out well
   B. advise him not to worry
   C. explain that the problem is quite a usual one and that the situation will be brighter soon
   D. give no opinion and change the subject when practicable

7. All of the following are generally good approaches for an interviewer to use in order to improve his interviews EXCEPT
   A. developing a routine approach so that interviews can be standardized
   B. comparing his procedure with that of others engaged in similar work
   C. reviewing each interview critically, picking out one or two weak points to concentrate on improving
   D. comparing his own more successful and less successful interviews

8. Assume that a supervisor suggests at a staff meeting that digital recorders be provided for interviewers. Following are four arguments *against* the use of digital recorders that are raised by other members of the staff that might be valid:
   I. Recorded interviews provide too much unnecessary information
   II. Recorded interviews provide no record of manner or gestures
   III. Digital recorders are too cumbersome and difficult for the average supervisor to manage
   IV. Digital recorders may inhibit the interviewee

Which one of the following choices MOST accurately classifies the above into those which are generally *invalid* and those which are *not*?
A. I and II are generally valid, but III and IV are not.
B. IV is generally valid, but I, II, and III are not.
C. I, II, and IV are generally valid, but III is not.
D. I, II, III, and IV are generally valid.

9. During an interview, the PRIMARY advantage of the technique of using questions as opposed to allowing the interviewee to talk freely is that questioning
   A. gives the interviewer greater control
   B. provides a more complete picture
   C. makes the interviewee more relaxed
   D. decreases the opportunity for exaggeration

10. Assume that, in conducting an interview, an interviewer takes into consideration the age, sex, education, and background of the subject.
    This practice is GENERALLY considered
    A. *undesirable*, mainly because an interviewer may be prejudiced by such factors
    B. *desirable*, mainly because these are factors which might influence a person's response to certain questions
    C. *undesirable*, mainly because these factors rarely have any bearing on the matter being investigated
    D. *desirable*, mainly because certain categories of people answer certain questions in the same way

11. If a client should begin to tell his life story during an interview, the BEST course of action for an interviewer to take is to
    A. interrupt immediately and insist that they return to business
    B. listen attentively until the client finishes and then ask if they can return to the subject
    C. pretend to have other business and come back later to see the client
    D. interrupt politely at an appropriate point and direct the client's attention to the subject

12. An interviewer who is trying to discover the circumstances surrounding a client's accident would be MOST successful during an interview if he avoided questions which
    A. lead the client to discuss the matter in detail
    B. can easily be answered by either "yes" or "no"
    C. ask for specific information
    D. may be embarrassing or annoying to the client

13. A client being interviewed may develop an emotional reaction (positive or negative) toward the interviewer.
    The BEST attitude for the interviewer to take toward such feelings is that they are
    A. *inevitable*; they should be accepted but kept under control
    B. *unusual*; they should be treated impersonally

C. *obstructive*; they should be resisted at all costs
D. *abnormal*; they should be eliminated as soon as possible

14. Encouraging the client being interviewed to talk freely at first is a technique that is supported by all of the following reasons EXCEPT that it
    A. tends to counteract any preconceived ideas that the interviewer may have entertained about the client
    B. gives the interviewer a chance to learn the best method of approach to obtain additional information
    C. inhibits the client from looking to the interviewer for support and advice
    D. allows the client to reveal the answers to many questions before they are asked

14.____

15. Of the following, generally the MOST effective way for an interviewer to assure full cooperation from the client he is interviewing is to
    A. sympathize with the client's problems and assure him of concern
    B. tell a few jokes before beginning to ask questions
    C. convince the patient that the answers to the questions will help him as well as the interviewer
    D. arrange the interview when the client feels best

15.____

16. Since many elderly people are bewildered and helpless when interviewed, special consideration should be given to them.
    Of the following, the BEST way for an interviewer to *initially* approach elderly clients who express anxiety and fear is to
    A. assure them that they have nothing to worry about
    B. listen patiently and show interest in them
    C. point out the specific course of action that is best for them
    D. explain to them that many people have overcome much greater difficulties

16.____

17. Assume that, in planning an initial interview, an interviewer determines in advance what information is needed in order to fulfill the purpose of the interview.
    Of the following, this procedure usually does NOT
    A. reduce the number of additional interviews required
    B. expedite the processing of the case
    C. improve public opinion of the interviewer's agency
    D. assure the cooperation of the person interviewed

17.____

18. Sometimes an interviewer deliberately introduces his own personal interests and opinions into an interview with a client.
    In general, this practice should be considered
    A. *desirable*, primarily because the relationship between client and interviewer becomes social rather than businesslike
    B. *undesirable*, primarily because the client might complain to his supervisor
    C. *desirable*, primarily because the focus of attention is directed toward the client
    D. *undesirable*, primarily because an argument between client and interviewer could result

18.____

19. The one of the following types of interviewees who presents the LEAST difficult problem to handle is the person who
    A. answers with a great many qualifications
    B. talks at length about unrelated subjects so that the interviewer cannot ask questions
    C. has difficulty understanding the interviewer's vocabulary
    D. breaks into the middle of sentences and completes them with a meaning of his own

    19.____

20. A man being interviewed is entitled to Medicaid, but he refuses to sign up for it because he says he cannot accept any form of welfare.
    Of the following, the BEST course of action for an interviewer to take FIRST is to
    A. try to discover the reason for his feeling this way
    B. tell him that he should be glad financial help is available
    C. explain that others cannot help him if he will not help himself
    D. suggest that he speak to someone who is already on Medicaid

    20.____

21. Of the following, the outcome of an interview by an interviewer depend MOST heavily on the
    A. personality of the interviewee
    B. personality of the interviewer
    C. subject matter of the questions asked
    D. interaction between interviewer and interviewee

    21.____

22. Some clients being interviewed by an interviewer are primarily interested in making a favorable impression.
    The interviewer should be aware of the fact that such clients are MORE likely than other clients to
    A. try to anticipate the answers the interviewer is looking for
    B. answer all questions openly and frankly
    C. try to assume the role of interviewer
    D. be anxious to get the interview over as quickly as possible

    22.____

23. The type of interview which a hospital care interviewer usually conducts is *substantially different* from most interviewing situations in all of the following EXCEPT the
    A. setting
    B. kinds of clients
    C. techniques employed
    D. kinds of problems

    23.____

24. During an interview, an interviewer uses a "leading question."
    This type of question is so-called because it *generally*
    A. starts a series of questions about one topic
    B. suggests the answer which the interviewer wants
    C. forms the basis for a following "trick" question
    D. sets, at the beginning, the tone of the interview

    24.____

25. An interviewer may face various difficulties when he tries to obtain information from a client.
Of the following, the difficulty which is EASIEST for the interviewer to overcome occurs when a client
   A. is unwilling to reveal the information
   B. misunderstands what information is needed
   C. does not have the information available to him
   D. is unable to coherently give the information requested

25._____

KEY (CORRECT ANSWERS)

1. C
2. B
3. C
4. C
5. D

6. D
7. A
8. C
9. A
10. B

11. D
12. B
13. A
14. C
15. C

16. B
17. D
18. D
19. C
20. A

21. D
22. A
23. C
24. B
25. B

TEST 2

DIRECTIONS: Each question or incomplete statement is followed by several suggested answers or completions. Select the one that BEST answers the question or completes the statement. *PRINT THE LETTER OF THE CORRECT ANSWER IN THE SPACE AT THE RIGHT.*

1. Of the following, the MOST appropriate manner for an interviewer to assume during an interview with a client is
   A. authoritarian   B. paternal   C. casual   D. businesslike

   1.____

2. The systematic study of interviewing theory, principles, and techniques by an interviewer will USUALLY
   A. aid him to act in a depersonalized manner
   B. turn his interviewees into stereotyped affairs
   C. make the people he interviews feel manipulated
   D. give him a basis for critically examining his own practice

   2.____

3. Compiling in advance a list of general questions to ask a client during an interview is a technique USUALLY considered
   A. *desirable*, chiefly because reference to the list will help keep the interview focused on the important issues
   B. *undesirable*, chiefly because use of such a list will discourage the client from speaking freely
   C. *desirable*, chiefly because the list will serve as a record of what questions were asked
   D. *undesirable*, chiefly because use of such a list will make the interview too mechanical and impersonal

   3.____

4. The one of the following which is usually of GREATEST importance in winning the cooperation of a person being interviewed and while achieving the purpose of the interview is the interviewer's ability to
   A. gain the confidence of the person being interviewed
   B. stick to the subject of the interview
   C. handle a person who is obviously lying
   D. prevent the person being interviewed from withholding information

   4.____

5. While interviewing clients, an interviewer should use the technique of interruption, beginning to speak when a client has temporarily paused at the end of a phrase or sentence, in order to
   A. limit the client's ability to voice his objections or complaints
   B. shorten, terminate or redirect a client's response
   C. assert authority when he feels that the client is too conceited
   D. demonstrate to the client that pauses in speech should be avoided

   5.____

6. An interviewer might gain background information about a client by being aware of the person's speech during an interview.
   Which one of the following patterns of speech would offer the LEAST accurate information about a client? The

   6.____

A. number of slang expressions and the level of vocabulary
B. presence and degree of an accent
C. rate of speech and the audibility level
D. presence of a physical speech defect

7. Suppose that you are interviewing a distressed client who claims that he was just laid off from his job and has no money to pay his rent.
   Your FIRST action should be to
   A. ask if he has sought other employment or has other sources of income
   B. express your sympathy but explain that he must pay the rent on time
   C. inquire about the reasons he was laid off from work
   D. try to transfer him to a smaller apartment which he can afford

7._____

8. Suppose you have some background information on an applicant whom you are interviewing. During the interview, it appears that the applicant is giving you false information.
   The BEST thing for you to do at that point is to
   A. pretend that you are not aware of the written facts and let him continue
   B. tell him what you already know and discuss the discrepancies with him
   C. terminate the interview and make a note that the applicant is untrustworthy
   D. tell him that, because he is making false statements, he will not be eligible for an apartment

8._____

9. A Spanish-speaking applicant may want to bring his bilingual child with him to an interview to act as an interpreter.
   Which of the following would be LEAST likely to affect the value of an interview in which an applicant's child has act as interpreter?
   A. It may make it undesirable to ask certain questions.
   B. A child may do an inadequate job of interpretation.
   C. A child's answers may indicate his feelings toward his parents.
   D. The applicant may not want to reveal all information in front of his child.

9._____

10. Assume you are assigned to interview applicants.
    Of the following, which is the BEST attitude for you to take in dealing with applicants?
    A. Assume they will enjoy being interviewed because they believe that you have the power of decision
    B. Expect that they have a history of anti-social behavior in the family, and probe deeply into the social development of family members
    C. Expect that they will try to control the interview, thus you should keep them on the defensive
    D. Assume that they will be polite and cooperative and attempt to secure the information you need in a business-like manner

10._____

11. If you are interviewing an applicant who is a minority group member in reference to his eligibility, it would be BEST for you to use language that is
    A. *informal*, using ethnic expressions known to the applicant
    B. *technical*, using the expressions commonly used in the agency

11._____

C. *simple*, using words and phrases which laymen understand
D. *formal* to remind the applicant that he is dealing with a government agency

12. When interviewing an applicant to determine his eligibility, it is MOST important to
    A. have a prior mental picture of the typical eligible applicant
    B. conduct the interview strictly according to a previously prepared script
    C. keep in mind the goal of the interview, which is to determine eligibility
    D. get an accurate and detailed account of the applicant's life history

13. The practice of trying to imagine yourself in the applicant's place during an interview is
    A. *good*, mainly because you will be able to evaluate his responses better
    B. *good*, mainly because it will enable you to treat him as a friend rather than as an applicant
    C. *poor*, mainly because it is important for the applicant to see you as an impartial person
    D. *poor*, mainly because it is too time-consuming to do this with each applicant

14. When dealing with clients from different ethnic backgrounds, you should be aware of certain tendencies toward prejudice.
    Which of the following statements is LEAST likely to be valid?
    A. Whites prejudiced against Blacks are more likely to be prejudiced against Hispanics than Whites not prejudiced against Blacks.
    B. The less a White is in competition with Blacks, the less likely he is to be prejudiced against them.
    C. Persons who have moved from one social group to another are likely to retain the attitudes and prejudices of their original social group.
    D. When there are few Blacks or Hispanics in a project, Whites are less likely to be prejudiced against them than when there are many.

15. Of the following, the one who is MOST likely to be a good interviewer of people seeking assistance, is one who
    A. tries to get applicants to apply to another agency instead
    B. believes that it is necessary to get as much pertinent information as possible in order to determine the applicant's real needs
    C. believes that people who seek assistance are likely to have persons with a history of irresponsible behavior in their households
    D. is convinced that there is no need for a request for assistance

KEY (CORRECT ANSWERS)

1.	D	6.	C	11.	C
2.	D	7.	A	12.	C
3.	A	8.	B	13.	A
4.	A	9.	C	14.	C
5.	B	10.	D	15.	B

READING COMPREHENSION
UNDERSTANDING AND INTERPRETING WRITTEN MATERIAL
EXAMINATION SECTION
TEST 1

DIRECTIONS: Each question or incomplete statement is followed by several suggested answers or completions. Select the one that BEST answers the question or completes the statement. *PRINT THE LETTER OF THE CORRECT ANSWER IN THE SPACE AT THE RIGHT.*

Questions 1-8.

DIRECTIONS: Questions 1 through 8 are to be answered on the basis of the following passage.

The child lives in a context which is itself neither simple nor unitary and which continuously affects his behavior and development. Patterns of stimulation come to him out of this context. In turn, by virtue of his own make-up, he selects from that context. At all times, there is a reciprocal relation between the human organism and his biosocial context. Because the child is limited in time, behavior becomes structured, and patterns develop both in the stimulus field and in his own response system. Some stimulus patterns become significant because they modify the developmental stream by affecting practice or social relations with others. Others remain insignificant because they do not affect this web of relations. Why one pattern is significant and another is not is a crucial problem for child psychology.

1. The author states that 1.____
    A. environmental forces have an important effect in determining both the child's actions and his course of growth
    B. environmental and hereditary forces play an equal part in determining both the child's actions and his course of growth
    C. even the environmental forces which are not consciously important to the child can affect both learning and personality
    D. the child's personality is shaped more by the total pattern of pressures in the environment

2. The author develops *context* so as to make it mean 2.____
    A. the nature of the child's immediate environment
    B. a complex rather than a simple home structure
    C. a multitude of past, present, and future forces
    D. internal as well as external influences

3. According to the author, the CRITICAL forces to be studied are those which 3.____
    A. are unconscious forces
    B. are conscious, unconscious, and subconscious forces
    C. cause the child to respond
    D. modify the child's interpersonal relationships

149

4. The author's point of view might BEST be labeled as
   A. environmentalist B. behaviorist
   C. psychobiosocial   D. gestaltist

5. The author maintains that the environment
   A. is relatively stable
   B. is in a constant state of flux
   C. shows periods of marked instability
   D. is more stable than unstable

6. From the above paragraph, it is to be inferred that the
   A. child's personality is mechanistically determined by the nature of the environment
   B. unique personality between the child and his environment shapes his personality
   C. child really shapes his own personality
   D. child's personality is more likely to be affected by than to affect the environment

7. By *structured behavior*, the author means
   A. conditioning of responses
   B. differentiated activity
   C. characteristic modes of reaction
   D. responses that have been modified by the developmental stream

8. The *patterns* to which the author refers are
   A. different for all children
   B. culturally determined mainly
   C. biologically determined mainly
   D. psychologically determined mainly

Questions 9-13.

DIRECTIONS: Questions 9 through 13 are to be answered on the basis of the following passage.

The Division of Child Guidance makes certain provisions for summer vacations for children receiving foster care. Foster parents wishing to take the child on a vacation within the United States must file Form CG-42 in duplicate at the office of the Division not later than 3 weeks prior to the starting date of the planned vacation. Such request must be approved in writing by the Social Investigator and the Assistant Supervisor. After the request has been approved, the original copy of Form CG-42 must be returned to the foster parents by the Social Investigator no later than 3 days prior to the planned starting date of the vacation. The city continues to pay the foster parents the standard rate for the child's care.

If the foster parents plan to take the child on a vacation outside the continental United States, Form CG-42 must be submitted in triplicate and must be received no later than 5 weeks prior to the starting date of the planned vacation. Such Form CG-42 for vacation outside the country must also be approved by the Case Supervisor. There will be no payment for time spent outside the United States.

When the approved original Form CG-42 is returned to the foster parents, it shall be accompanied by an original copy of Form CG-43. A duplicate copy of Form CG-43 shall be forwarded by the Case Supervisor to the Children's Accounts Section to stop payment for time expected to be spent outside the United States.

9. When a foster parent plans to take his foster child on a vacation trip, the Division of Child Guidance must receive Form   9._____
    A. CG-42 in triplicate no later than five weeks prior to the scheduled start of his vacation trip to Canada
    B. CG-42 in triplicate no later than three weeks prior to the scheduled start of his vacation trip to Mexico
    C. CG-43 in triplicate no later than three weeks prior to the scheduled start of the vacation trip to Arizona
    D. CG-43 in duplicate no later than five weeks prior to the scheduled start of his vacation trip regardless of location

10. The one of the following steps which is required in processing a request from a foster parent to take a child on a vacation trip is that the   10._____
    A. Case Supervisor send the original copy of Form CG-42 to the appropriate section in the case of a child who will spend all his vacation in a foreign country
    B. Children's Accounts Section receive the duplicate copy of Form CG-43 in the case of a child who will spend any part of his vacation in a foreign country
    C. Division of Child Guidance keep a permanent file of original copies of Form CG-43 to keep a control of all current vacation requests
    D. foster parents receive the triplicate copy of Form CG-42 from the Social Investigator in the case of a child who will spend part of his vacation in the United States

11. When a foster child spends an approved vacation with his foster father, payment for the child's care will be given to the foster father for   11._____
    A. none of the time if part of the vacation is spent in a foreign country
    B. that part of the vacation spent inside the United States but a reduced daily rate
    C. the entire period at a standard rate if the vacation is spent wholly in the United States
    D. the entire time regardless of whether or not it is spent in a foreign country

12. The Division of Child Guidance must notify a foster parent that his request to take his foster child on a vacation outside the country has been approved by sending him the approved _____ copy of Form CG-42 and _____ copy of CG-43.   12._____
    A. duplicate; duplicate
    B. duplicate; original
    C. original; duplicate
    D. original; original

151

13. On the basis of the above passage, children receiving foster care may be taken 13.____
on a vacation trip by their foster parents to a location
   A. anywhere in the world with the written approval of the Social Investigator only
   B. of the foster parents' choosing but only with the written approval of both the Assistant Supervisor and Case Supervisor
   C. outside the United States but only with the written approval of the Social Investigator, Assistant Supervisor, and Case Supervisor
   D. within the United States with the written approval of the Case Supervisor only

Questions 14-18.

DIRECTIONS: Questions 14 through 18 are statements based on the following paragraphs. For each question, there are two statements.
Based on the information in the paragraphs, mark your answer:
A. if only statement I is correct;
B. if only statement II is correct;
C. if both statements are correct.
Mark your answer D if the excerpts do not contain sufficient evidence for concluding whether either or both statements are correct.

Almost 49,000 children were living in foster family homes or voluntary institutions in the state at the end of 2003. These were children whose parents or relatives were unable or unwilling to care for them in their own homes. The State Department of Social Services supervised the care of these children served under the auspices of 64 social services districts and more than 150 private agencies and institutions. Almost 8 out of every 1,000 children 18 years of age or younger were in care away from their homes at the end of 2003. This estimate does not include a substantial, but unknown, number of children living outside their own homes who were placed there by their parents, relatives, or others without the assistance of a social agency.

The number of children in care (dependent, neglected, and delinquent combined) was up by 4,500 or 10 percent over the 2000-2003 period. Both the city and state reported similar increases. In the comparable period, the state's child population (18 years or less) rose only three percent. Thus, the foster care rate showed a moderate increase to 7.7 per thousand in 2003 from 7.2 thousand in 2000. The city's foster care rate in 2003, at 10.5 per thousand, was almost twice that for upstate New York, 5.7 per thousand. (Excluding delinquent children from the total care in the state reduces the foster care rate per thousand to 7.2 in 2003 and the comparable 2000 figure to 6.7.)

Dependent and neglected children made up about 95 percent of the total number in foster family homes and voluntary institutions in the state at the end of 2003, as they did in 2000. Delinquent children sent into care (outside the state training school system) by the Family Court accounted for only 5 percent of the total. The number of delinquent children in care rose 5 percent, as an increase in the state, 28 percent, more than offset a 13 percent decline in the city. Delinquents comprised 4.9 percent of the total number of children in care upstate at the end of 2003 and 3.9 percent in the city.

14. I. There were 45,000 children in care away from their own homes over the 2000-2003 period.
    II. The percentage decline of delinquent children in care in the city in 2003 was offset by a greater increase in the rest of the state.

14.____

15. I. The increase in delinquent care in the state from 2000 to 2003 cannot be determined from the data given.
    II. The state's foster care rate in 2003, exclusive of the city, was about one-half the rate for the city

15.____

16. I. In 2000 and in 2003, the percentage of dependent and neglected children in foster family homes and voluntary institutions in the state was about the same
    II. In 2000, the number of dependent and neglected children in foster family homes and voluntary institutions in the state was 43,250

16.____

17. I. The city's child population rose approximately three percent from 2000 to 2003.
    II. At the end of 2003, less than 1% of the children 18 years of age or younger were in care.

17.____

18. I. Delinquents in the city comprised 4.4 percent of the total number of children in care in the city at the end of 2000.
    II. An unsubstantial number of children living outside their own homes were placed by their parents or relatives without the assistance of a social agency.

18.____

Questions 19-25.

DIRECTIONS: Questions 19 through 25 are to be answered SOLELY on the basis of the information contained in the following paragraph. Each question consists of a statement. You are to indicate whether the statement is TRUE (T) or FALSE (F).

RESPONSIBILITY OF PARENTS

In a recent survey, ninety percent of the people interviewed felt that parents should be held responsible for the delinquency of their children. Forty-eight out of fifty states have laws holding parents criminally responsible for contributing to the delinquency of their children. It is generally accepted that parents are a major influence in the early moral development of their children. Yet, in spite of all this evidence, practical experience seems to prove that *punish the parents* laws are wrong. Legally, there is some question about the constitutionality of such laws. How far can one person be held responsible for the actions of another? Further, although there are many such laws, the fact remains that they are rarely used and where they are used, they fail in most cases to accomplish the end for which they were intended.

19. Nine out of ten of those interviewed held that parents should be responsible for the delinquency of their children.

19.____

20. Forty-eight percent of the states have laws holding parents responsible for contributing to the delinquency of their children.   20._____

21. Most people feel that parents have little influence on the early moral development of their children.   21._____

22. Experience seems to indicate that laws holding parents responsible for children's delinquency are wrong.   22._____

23. There is no doubt that laws holding parents responsible for delinquency of their children are within the Constitution.   23._____

24. Laws holding parents responsible for delinquent children are not often enforced.   24._____

25. *Punish the parent* laws usually achieve their purpose.   25._____

KEY (CORRECT ANSWERS)

1.	A		11.	C
2.	D		12.	D
3.	D		13.	C
4.	C		14.	B
5.	B		15.	B
6.	B		16.	A
7.	C		17.	D
8.	A		18.	D
9.	A		19.	T
10.	B		20.	F

21. F
22. T
23. F
24. T
25. F

TEST 2

DIRECTIONS: Each question or incomplete statement is followed by several suggested answers or completions. Select the one that BEST answers the question or completes the statement. *PRINT THE LETTER OF THE CORRECT ANSWER IN THE SPACE AT THE RIGHT.*

Questions 1-3.

DIRECTIONS: Questions 1 through 3 are to be answered SOLELY on the basis of the following passage.

    Undoubtedly, the ultimate solution to the housing problem of the hard-core slum does not lie in code enforcement, however defined. The only solution to that problem is demolition, clearance, and new construction. However, it is also clear that, even with government assistance, new construction is not keeping pace with the obsolescence and deterioration of the existing housing inventory of our cities. Add to this the facts of an increasing population and the continuing migration into metropolitan areas, as well as the demands for more and better housing that grow out of continuing economic prosperity and high employment, and some intimation may be gained of the dimensions of the problem of maintaining our housing supply so that it may begin to meet the need.

1. The one of the following that would be the MOST appropriate title for the above passage is
    A. PROBLEMS ASSOCIATED WITH MAINTAINING AN ADEQUATE HOUSING SUPPLY
    B. DEMOLITION AS A REMEDY FOR HOUSING PROBLEMS
    C. GOVERNMENT'S ESSENTIAL ROLE IN CODE ENFORCEMENT
    D. THE ULTIMATE SOLUTION TO THE HARD-CORE SLUM PROBLEM

1.____

2. According to the above passage, housing code enforcement is
    A. a way to encourage local initiative in urban renewal
    B. a valuable tool that has fallen into disuse
    C. inadequate as a solution to slum housing problems
    D. responsible for some of the housing problems since the code has not been adequately defined

2.____

3. The above passage makes it clear that the BASIC solution to the housing problem is to
    A. erect new buildings after demolition and site clearance
    B. discourage migration into the metropolitan area
    C. increase rents paid to landlords
    D. enforce the housing code strictly

3.____

Questions 4-5.

DIRECTIONS: Questions 4 and 5 are to be answered on the basis of the following passage.

Under common law, the tenant was obliged to continue to pay rent, at the risk of eviction, regardless of the condition of the premises. This obligation was based on the following established common law principles: first, that in the absence of express agreement, a lease does not contain any implied warrant of fitness or habitability; second, that the person in possession of premises has the obligation to repair and maintain them; and third, that a lease conveys an interest in real estate rather than binding one to a mutual obligation. Once having conveyed his property, the landlord's right to rent was unconditional. Thus, even if he made an express agreement to repair, the landlord's right to rent remained independent of his promise to repair. This doctrine, known as the *independence of covenant*, required the tenant to continue to pay rent or risk eviction, and to bring a separate action against the landlord for damages resulting from his breach of agreement to repair.

4. According to the above passage, common law provided that a lease would   4.____
    A. bar an ex parte action
    B. bind the parties thereto to a reciprocal obligation
    C. provide an absolute defense for breach of agreement
    D. transmit an interest in real property

5. According to the above passage, the *independence of covenants* required that   5.____
   the
    A. tenant continue to pay rent even for unfit housing
    B. landlord hold rents in escrow for aggrieved tenants
    C. landlord show valid cause for non-performance of lease requirements
    D. tenant surrender the demised premises in improved condition

Questions 6-11.

DIRECTIONS: Questions 6 through 11 are to be answered SOLELY on the basis of the information given in the following passage.

The City of X has set up a Maximum Base Rent Program for all rent-controlled apartments. The objective is to insure that the landlord will get a fair, but not excessive, profit on his building to stem the great tide of buildings being abandoned by their owners, and to encourage landlords to continue the upkeep of their property. The Maximum Base Rent Program permits the landlord to raise rents under carefully devised standards, while practically no raises in rents in this City were permitted under previous guidelines.

Under this plan, the City determines a Maximum Base Rent amount by means of a formula which takes into account the age of the building, the number of apartments, total rents received from the building, the amount of expenses, and labor costs. The Maximum Base Rent amount is to be recomputed every two year to allow for increases or decreases in building costs.

The Maximum Base Rent, which will allow the landlord to make a *fair return* on his investment, may not be collected immediately, however, since no rent increases over 7.5 percent will be permitted in any one year. The highest actual rent for each apartment during a given year will be called the Maximum Collectible Rent. This will be computed so that the increase over the present rent is not more than 7.5 percent ($7.50 on every $100.00). Sometimes, it may be less. Therefore, collectible rents will increase each year until the Maximum Base Rent is reached.

6. According to the above passage, the Maximum Base Rent is determined by the   6.____
   A. landlord
   B. Mayor
   C. Rent Commissioner
   D. City

7. Which of the following, according to the above passage, permits a *fair return*   7.____
   on the landlord's investment?
   The_____ Rent Program.
   A. Minimum Base
   B. Maximum Bass
   C. Minimum Collectible
   D. Maximum Collectible

8. It may be concluded from the above passage that the City of X hopes that   8.____
   insuring fair profits for landlords will be followed by
   A. good upkeep of apartment buildings
   B. decreased interest rates on home mortgages
   C. lower rents in the future
   D. a better formula for determining rents

9. According to the above passage, guidelines for determining rents previous to   9.____
   the Maximum Base Rent Program resulted in
   A. practically no raises in rents being made
   B. rent increases of approximately 10 percent a year
   C. a *fair return* to landlords from most rents
   D. landlords making too much money on their property

10. Based on the above passage, which is the MOST correct description of the   10.____
    kinds of facts that are taken into consideration when determining the Maximum
    Base Rent?
    Facts about
    A. labor costs and politics
    B. the landlord and labor costs
    C. the building and labor costs
    D. the building and the landlord

11. According to the above passage, the MAXIMUM annual increase in rent for   11.____
    a tenant in rent-controlled housing under the Maximum Base Rent Program is
    A. 7.5 percent each year for ten years
    B. 7.5 percent each year until the Maximum Base Rent is reached
    C. always under 7.5 percent a year
    D. $7.50 each year until it reaches $100.00

Questions 12-15.

DIRECTIONS: Questions 12 through 15 are to be answered SOLELY on the basis of the information contained in the following paragraph.

In all projects (except sites), when the Manager determines that a vacant apartment is to be permanently removed from the rent roll for any reason, e.g., the apartment has been converted to an office or community space, he shall notify the cashier by memorandum. The cashier shall enter the reduction in dwelling units in the Rent Control Book as of the first of the month following the date on which the apartment was vacated. He shall also prepare a reduction in Rent Roll (Form 105.046), the original of which is to be attached to the file copy of the Project Monthly Summary for the month during which the reduction is effective. Copies are to be sent to the Finance and Audit Department, Budget Section, and to the Chief of Insurance.

12. The purpose of the above paragraph is to provide for a procedure in handling 12.____
    A. the accounting for space occupied by offices and community centers
    B. apartments not rented as of the first of the month following the date on which the apartment was vacated
    C. vacant apartment temporarily used as office space
    D. vacant apartment permanently removed from the rent roll

13. The Rent Control Book is a control on the amount of monthly rents charged. 13.____
    According to the above paragraph, another function of the Rent Control Book is to indicate the
    A. number of offices and community spaces available in the project
    B. number of dwelling units in the project
    C. number of vacant apartments in the project
    D. rental loss for all offices and community spaces

14. In accordance with the above paragraph, the original of the Form 105.046 is to be 14.____
    A. sent to Central Office with the Project Monthly Summary
    B. kept in the project files with the project copy of the Project Monthly Summary
    C. sent to the Finance and Audit Department
    D. sent to the Chief of Insurance

15. The MOST likely reason for informing the Chief of Insurance of the removal of an apartment from the rent roll is to notify him 15.____
    A. to make adjustments in the insurance coverage
    B. of a future change in the address of the office or community space
    C. of a change in the project rent income
    D. of a possible increase in the number of project employees

Questions 16-20.

DIRECTIONS: Questions 16 through 20 are to be answered SOLELY on the basis of the information provided in the following passage.

It is the Housing Administration's policy that all tenants, whether new or transferring from one housing development to another, should be required to pay a standard security deposit of one month's rent based on the rent at the time of admission. There are, however, certain exceptions to this policy. Employees of the Administration shall not be required to pay a security deposit if they secure an apartment in an Administration development. Where the payment of a full security deposit may present a hardship to a tenant, the development's manager may allow a tenant to move into an apartment upon payment of only part of the security deposit. In such cases, however, the tenant must agree to gradually pay the balance of the deposit. If a tenant transfers from one apartment to another within the same project, the security deposit originally paid by the tenant for his former apartment will be acceptable for his new apartment, even if the rent in the new apartment is greater than the rent in the former one. Finally, tenants who receive public assistance need not pay a security deposit before moving into an apartment if the appropriate agency states, in writing, that it will pay the deposit. However, it is the responsibility of the development's manager to make certain that payment shall be received within one month of the date that the tenant moves into the apartment.

16. According to the above passage, when a tenant transfers from one apartment to another in the same development, the Housing Administration will
    A. accept the tenant's old security deposit as the security deposit for his new apartment regardless of the new apartment's rent
    B. refund the tenant's old security deposit and not require him to pay a new deposit
    C. keep the tenant's old security deposit and require him to pay a new deposit
    D. require the tenant to pay a new security deposit based on the difference between his old rent and his new rent

16.____

17. On the basis of the above passage, it is INCORRECT to state that a tenant who receives public assistance may move into an Administration development if
    A. he pays the appropriate security deposit
    B. the appropriate agency gives a written indication that it will pay the security deposit before the tenant moves in
    C. the appropriate agency states, by telephone, that it will pay the security deposit
    D. the appropriate agency writes the manager to indicate that the security deposit will be paid within one month but not less than two weeks from the date the tenant moves into the apartment

17.____

18. On the basis of the above passage, a tenant who transfers from an apartment in one development to an apartment in a different development will
    A. forfeit his old security deposit and be required to pay another deposit
    B. have his old security deposit refunded and not have to pay a new deposit
    C. pay the difference between his old security deposit and the new one
    D. have to pay a security deposit based on the new apartment's rent

18.____

19. The Housing Administration will NOT require payment of a security deposit if a tenant
    A. is an Administration employee
    B. is receiving public assistance
    C. claims that payment will present a hardship
    D. indicates, in writing, that he will be responsible for any damage done to his apartment

19.____

20. Of the following, the BEST title for the above passage is: 20.____
    A. SECURITY DEPOSITS – TRANSFERS
    B. SECURITY DEPOSITS – POLICY
    C. EXEMPTIONS AND EXCEPTIONS – SECURITY DEPOSITS
    D. AMOUNTS – SECURITY DEPOSITS

Questions 21-23.

DIRECTIONS: Questions 21 through 23 are to be answered SOLELY on the basis of the following paragraphs.

    In our program, we must continually strive to increase public good will and to maintain that good will which we have already established. It is important to remember in all your public contacts that to a good many people you are the Department. Don't take out any of your personal gripes on the public. When we must appeal to the public for cooperation, that is when any good will we have built up will come in handy. If the public has been given incorrect or incomplete help when seeking information or advice, or have received what they considered poor treatment in dealing with members of the Department, they will not provide a sympathetic audience when we direct our appeals to them.
    One of the Department activities in which there is considerable contact with the public is inspection. Any activity in this area poses special problems and makes your personal dealings with the individuals involved very important. You must bear in mind that you are dealing with people who are sensitive to the manner in which they are treated and you should guide yourself accordingly.
    Let us consider some of the aspects of the actual inspection of the premises:

    APPEARANCE: Your appearance will determine the initial impression made on anyone you deal with. It is often difficult to change a person's first impression, so try to make it a favorable one. Be neat and clean, show that you have taken some trouble to make a good appearance. Your appearance should form a part of a business-like attitude that should govern your inspection of any premises.

    APPROACH: Be courteous at all times. When you enter a building, immediately seek out the owner or occupant and ask his permission to inspect the premises. Ask him to accompany you on the inspection if he has the time, and explain to him the reasons why such inspections are made. Try to give him the feeling that this is a cooperative effort and that his part in this effort is appreciated. Do not make your approach on the basis that it is your legal right to inspect the premises; a <u>coercive</u> attitude tends to produce a hostile reaction.

21. Of the following, the BEST title for the subject covered in the above paragraphs is 21.____
    A. GOOD MANNERS   B. PUBLIC RELATIONS
    C. NEATNESS   D. INSPECTIONAL DUTIES

22. According to the above paragraph, the FIRST impression an inspector makes on the public is that of 22.____
    A. sympathy   B. courtesy
    C. cleanliness and dress   D. business attitude

23. According to the above paragraphs, if you want the public to cooperate with you, 23.____
you must
   A. be available at all times
   B. be sure that any information you give them is correct
   C. make sure that their complaints are justified
   D. be stern in your dealings with landlords

Questions 24-25.

DIRECTIONS: Questions 24 and 25 are to be answered SOLELY on the basis of the following passage.

There is no simple solution for controlling crime and deviant behavior. There is no panacea for anti-social conduct. The sooner society gives up the search for a single control solution, the sooner society will be able to face up to the immensity of the task and the never-ending responsibility of our social structure.

24. Which of the following statements is BEST supported by the above passage? 24.____
   A. Although crime causation may be considered singular, crime control is many-faceted.
   B. When society faces up to the immensity of the crime problem, it will find a single solution to it.
   C. A multi-faceted approach to crime control is better than trying to find a single cause or cure.
   D. Our social structure is responsible for a continuing search for a simple solution to anti-social behavior.

25. The crime problem can be solved when 25.____
   A. it is realized that no solution exists
   B. the problem is specifically identified
   C. criminals are punished
   D. none of the above

KEY (CORRECT ANSWERS)

1.	A	11.	B
2.	C	12.	D
3.	A	13.	B
4.	D	14.	B
5.	A	15.	A
6.	D	16.	A
7.	B	17.	C
8.	A	18.	D
9.	A	19.	A
10.	C	20.	B

21. B
22. C
23. B
24. C
25. D

PREPARING WRITTEN MATERIAL

PARAGRAPH REARRANGEMENT
COMMENTARY

The sentences that follow are in scrambled order. You are to rearrange them in proper order and indicate the letter choice containing the correct answer at the space at the right.

Each group of sentences in this section is actually a paragraph presented in scrambled order. Each sentence in the group has a place in that paragraph; no sentence is to be left out. You are to read each group of sentences and decide upon the best order in which to put the sentences so as to form a well-organized paragraph.

The questions in this section measure the ability to solve a problem when all the facts relevant to its solution are not given.

More specifically, certain positions of responsibility and authority require the employee to discover connection between events sometimes, apparently, unrelated. In order to do this, the employee will find it necessary to correctly infer that unspecified events have probably occurred or are likely to occur. This ability becomes especially important when action must be taken on incomplete information.

Accordingly, these questions require competitors to choose among several suggested alternatives, each of which presents a different sequential arrangement of the events. Competitors must choose the MOST logical of the suggested sequences.

In order to do so, they may be required to draw on general knowledge to infer missing concepts or events that are essential to sequencing the given events. Competitors should be careful to infer only what is essential to the sequence. The plausibility of the wrong alternatives will always require the inclusion of unlikely events or of additional chains of events which are NOT essential to sequencing the given events.

It's very important to remember that you are looking for the best of the four possible choices, and that the best choice of all may not even be one of the answers you're given to choose from.

There is no one right way to solve these problems. Many people have found it helpful to first write out the order of the sentences, as they would have arranged them, on their scrap paper before looking at the possible answers. If their optimum answer is there, this can save them some time. If it isn't, this method can still give insight into solving the problem. Others find it most helpful to just go through each of the possible choices, contrasting each as they go along. You should use whatever method feels comfortable and works for you.

While most of these types of questions are not that difficult, we've added a higher percentage of the difficult type, just to give you more practice. Usually there are only one or two questions on this section that contain such subtle distinctions that you're unable to answer confidently. And you then may find yourself stuck deciding between two possible choices, neither of which you're sure about.

EXAMINATION SECTION

TEST 1

DIRECTIONS: The sentences that follow are in scrambled order. You are to rearrange them in proper order and indicate the letter choice containing the correct answer. *PRINT THE LETTER OF THE CORRECT ANSWER IN THE SPACE AT THE RIGHT.*

1. Below are four statements labeled W, X, Y and Z. 1.____
    W. He was a strict and fanatic drillmaster.
    X. The word is always used in a derogatory sense and generally shows resentment and anger on the part of the user.
    Y. It is from the name of this Frenchman that we derive our English word, martinet.
    Z. Jean Martinet was the Inspector-General of Infantry during the reign of King Louis XIV.
    The PROPER order in which these sentences should be placed in a paragraph is:
    A. X, Z, W, Y   B. X, Z, Y, W   C. Z, W, Y, X   D. Z, Y, W, X

2. In the following paragraph, the sentences, which are numbered, have been jumbled. 2.____
    I. Since then it has undergone changes.
    II. It was incorporated in 1955 under the laws of the State of New York.
    III. Its primary purposes, a cleaner city, has, however, remained the same.
    IV. The Citizens Committee works in cooperation with the Mayor's Inter-departmental Committee for a Clean City. 3.____
    The order in which these sentences should be arranged to form a well-organized paragraph is:
    A. II, IV, I, III   B. III, IV, I, II   C. IV, II, I, III   D. IV, III, II, I

Questions 3-5.

DIRECTIONS: The sentences listed below are part of a meaningful paragraph but they are not given in their proper order. You are to decide what would be the BEST order in which to put the sentences so as to form a well-organized paragraph. Each sentence has a place in the paragraph; there are no extra sentences. You are then to answer Questions 3 through 5 inclusive on the basis of your rearrangements of these scrambled sentences into a properly organized paragraph.

In 1887 some insurance companies organized an Inspection Department to advise their clients on all phases of fire prevention and protection. Probably this has been due to the smaller annual fire losses in Great Britain than in the United States. It tests various fire prevention devices and appliances and determines manufacturing hazards and their safeguards. Fire research began earlier in the United States and is more advanced than in Great Britain. Later they established a laboratory specializing in electrical, mechanical, hydraulic, and chemical fields.

3. When the five sentences are arranged in proper order, the paragraph starts with the sentence which begins
   A. "In 1887..."   B. "Probably this..."   C. "It tests..."
   D. "Fire research..."   E. "Later they..."

4. In the last sentence listed above, "they" refers to
   A. the insurance companies   B. the United States and Great Britain
   C. the Inspection Department   D. clients
   E. technicians

5. When the above paragraph is properly arranged, it ends with the words
   A. "...and protection."   B. "...the United States."
   C. "...their safeguards."   D. "...in Great Britain."
   E. "...chemical fields."

KEY (CORRECT ANSWERS)

1. C
2. C
3. D
4. A
5. C

TEST 2

DIRECTIONS: In each of the questions numbered I through V, several sentences are given. For each question, choose as your answer the group of number that represents the MOST logical order of these sentences if they were arranged in paragraph form. *PRINT THE LETTER OF THE CORRECT ANSWER IN THE SPACE AT THE RIGHT.*

1. I. It is established when one shows that the landlord has prevented the tenant's enjoyment of his interest in the property leased.
    II. Constructive eviction is the result of a breach of the covenant of quiet enjoyment implied in all leases.
    III. In some parts of the United States, it is not complete until the tenant vacates within a reasonable time.
    IV. Generally, the acts must be of such serious and permanent character as to deny the tenant the enjoyment of his possessing rights.
    V. In this event, upon abandonment of the premises, the tenant's liability for that ceases.
    The CORRECT answer is:
    A. II, I, IV, III, V
    B. V, II, III, I, IV
    C. IV, III, I, II, V
    D. I, III, V, IV, II

    1.____

2. I. The powerlessness before private and public authorities that is the typical experience of the slum tenant is reminiscent of the situation of blue-collar workers all through the nineteenth century.
    II. Similarly, in recent years, this chapter of history has been reopened by anti-poverty groups which have attempted to organize slum tenants to enable them to bargain collectively with their landlords about the conditions of their tenancies.
    III. It is familiar history that many of the worker remedied their condition by joining together and presenting their demands collectively.
    IV. Like the workers, tenants are forced by the conditions of modern life into substantial dependence on these who possess great political aid and economic power.
    V. What's more, the very fact of dependence coupled with an absence of education and self-confidence makes them hesitant and unable to stand up for what they need from those in power.
    The CORRECT answer is:
    A. V, IV, I, II, III
    B. II, III, I, V, IV
    C. III, I, V, IV, II
    D. I, IV, V, III, II

    2.____

3. I. A railroad, for example, when not acting as a common carrier may contract away responsibility for its own negligence.
    II. As to a landlord, however, no decision has been found relating to the legal effect of a clause shifting the statutory duty of repair to the tenant.
    III. The courts have not passed on the validity of clauses relieving the landlord of this duty and liability.
    IV. They have, however, upheld the validity of exculpatory clauses in other types of contracts.

    3.____

167

V. Housing regulations impose a duty upon the landlord to maintain leased premises in safe condition.
VI. As another example, a bailee may limit his liability except for gross negligence, willful acts, or fraud.

The CORRECT answer is:
A. II, I, VI, IV, III, V
B. I, III, IV, V, VI, II
C. III, V, I, IV, II, VI
D. V, III, IV, I, VI, II

4. I. Since there are only samples in the building, retail or consumer sales are generally eschewed by mart occupants, and in some instances, rigid controls are maintained to limit entrance to the mart only to those persons engaged in retailing.
    II. Since World War I, in many larger cities, there has developed a new type of property, called the mart building.
    III. It can, therefore, be used by wholesalers and jobbers for the display of sample merchandise.
    IV. This type of building is most frequently a multi-storied, finished interior property which is a cross between a retail arcade and a loft building.
    V. This limitation enables the mart occupants to ship the orders from another location after the retailer or dealer makes his selection from the samples.

    The CORRECT answer is:
    A. II, IV, III, I, V
    B. IV, III, V, I, II
    C. I, III, II, IV, V
    D. I, IV, II, III, V

5. I. In general, staff-line friction reduces the distinctive contribution of staff personnel.
    II. The conflicts, however, introduce an uncontrolled element into the managerial system.
    III. On the other hand, the natural resistance of the line to staff innovations probably usefully restrains over-eager efforts to apply untested procedures on a large scale.
    IV. Under such conditions, it is difficult to know when valuable ideas are being sacrificed.
    V. The relatively weak position of staff, requiring accommodation to the line, tends to restrict their ability to engage in free, experimental innovation.

    The CORRECT answer is:
    A. IV, II, III, I, V
    B. I, V, III, II, IV
    C. V, III, I, II, IV
    D. II, I, IV, V, III

KEY (CORRECT ANSWERS)

1. A
2. D
3. D
4. A
5. B

TEST 3

DIRECTIONS: Questions 1 through 4 consist of six sentences which can be arranged in a logical sequence. For each question, select the choice which places the numbered sentences in the MOST logical sequent. *PRINT THE LETTER OF THE CORRECT ANSWER IN THE SPACE AT THE RIGHT.*

1.
   I. The burden of proof as to each issue is determined before trial and remains upon the same party throughout the trial.
   II. The jury is at liberty to believe one witness' testimony as against a number of contradictory witnesses.
   III. In a civil case, the party bearing the burden of proof is required to prove his contention by a fair preponderance of the evidence.
   IV. However, it must be noted that a fair preponderance of evidence does not necessarily mean a greater number of witnesses.
   V. The burden of proof is the burden which rests upon one of the parties to an action to persuade the trier of the facts, generally the jury, that a proposition he asserts is true.
   VI. If the evidence is equally balanced, or if it leaves the jury in such doubt as to be unable to decide the controversy either way, judgment must be given against the party upon whom the burden of proof rests.
   The CORRECT answer is:
   A. III, II, V, IV, I, VI
   B. I, II, VI, V, III, IV
   C. III, IV, V, I, II, VI
   D. V, I, III, VI, IV, II

   1.____

2.
   I. If a parent is without assets and is unemployed, he cannot be convicted of the crime of non-support of a child.
   II. The term "sufficient ability" has been held to mean sufficient financial ability.
   III. It does not matter if his unemployment is by choice or unavoidable circumstances.
   IV. If he fails to take any steps at all, he may be liable to prosecution for endangering the welfare of a child.
   V. Under the penal law, a parent is responsible for the support of his minor child only if the parent is "of sufficient ability."
   VI. An indigent parent may meet his obligation by borrowing money or by seeking aid under the provisions of the Social Welfare Law.
   The CORRECT answer is:
   A. VI, I, V, III, II, IV
   B. I, III, V, II, IV, VI
   C. V, II, I, III, VI, IV
   D. I, VI, IV, V, II, III

   2.____

3.
   I. Consider, for example, the case of a rabble rouser who urges a group of twenty people to go out and break the windows of a nearby factory.
   II. Therefore, the law fills the indicated gap with the crime of inciting to riot.
   III. A person is considered guilty of inciting to riot when he urges ten or more persons to engage in tumultuous and violent conduct of a kind likely to create public alarm.
   IV. However, if he has not obtained the cooperation of at least four people, he cannot be charged with unlawful assembly.

   3.____

169

V. The charge of inciting to riot was added to the law to cover types of conduct which cannot be classified as either the crime of "riot" or the crime of "unlawful assembly."
VI. If he acquires the acquiescence of at least four of them, he is guilty of unlawful assembly even if the project does not materialize.
The CORRECT answer is:
A. III, V, I, VI, IV, II
B. V, I, IV, VI, II, III
C. III, IV, I, V, II, VI
D. V, I, IV, VI, III, II

4. I. If, however, the rebuttal evidence presents an issue of credibility, it is for the jury to determine whether the presumption has, in fact, been destroyed.
II. Once sufficient evidence to the contrary is introduced, the presumption disappears from the trial.
III. The effect of a presumption is to place the burden upon the adversary to come forward with evidence to rebut the presumption.
IV. When a presumption is overcome and ceases to exist in the case, the fact or facts which gave rise to the presumption still remain.
V. Whether a presumption has been overcome is ordinarily a question for the court.
VI. Such information may furnish a basis for a logical inference.
The CORRECT answer is:
A. IV, VI, II, V, I, III
B. III, II, V, I, IV, VI
C. V, III, VI, IV, II, I
D. V, IV, I, II, VI, III

KEY (CORRECT ANSWERS)

1. D
2. C
3. A
4. B

PREPARING WRITTEN MATERIAL
EXAMINATION SECTION
TEST 1

DIRECTIONS: Each question consists of a sentence which may or may not be an example of good English usage. Examine each sentence, considering grammar, punctuation, spelling, capitalization, and awkwardness. Then choose the correct statement about it from the four choices below it. If the English usage in the sentence given is better than any of the changes suggested in choices B, C, or D, pick choice A. (Do not pick a choice that will change the meaning of the sentence.) *PRINT THE LETTER OF THE CORRECT ANSWER IN THE SPACE AT THE RIGHT.*

1. We attended a staff conference on Wednesday the new safety and fire rules were discussed.
   A. This is an example of acceptable writing.
   B. The words "safety," "fire," and "rules" should begin with capital letters.
   C. There should be a comma after the word "Wednesday."
   D. There should be a period after the word "Wednesday" and the word "the" should begin with a capital letter.

1._____

2. Neither the dictionary or the telephone directory could be found in the office library.
   A. This is an example of acceptable writing.
   B. The word "or" should be changed to "nor."
   C. The word "library" should be spelled "libery."
   D. The word "neither" should be changed to "either."

2._____

3. The report would have been typed correctly if the typist could read the draft.
   A. This is an example of acceptable writing.
   B. The word "would" should be removed.
   C. The word "have" should be inserted after the word "could."
   D. The word "correctly" should be changed to "correct."

3._____

4. The supervisor brought the reports and forms to an employees desk.
   A. This is an example of acceptable writing.
   B. The word "brought" should be changed to "took."
   C. There should be a comma after the word "reports" and a comma after the word "forms."
   D. The word "employees" should be spelled "employee's."

4._____

5. It's important for all the office personnel to submit their vacation schedules on time.
   A. This is an example of acceptable writing.
   B. The word "It's" should be spelled "Its."
   C. The word "their" should be spelled "they're."
   D. The word "personnel" should be spelled "personal."

5._____

6. The report, along with the accompanying documents, were submitted for review.   6._____
   A. This is an example of acceptable writing.
   B. The words "were submitted" should be changed to "was submitted."
   C. The word "accompanying" should be spelled "accompaning."
   D. The comma after the word "report" should be taken out.

7. If others must use your files, be certain that they understand how the system works, but insist that you do all the filing and refiling.   7._____
   A. This is an example of acceptable writing.
   B. There should be a period after the word "works," and the word "but" should start a new sentence.
   C. The words "filing" and "refiling" should be spelled "fileing" and "refileing."
   D. There should be a comma after the word "but."

8. The appeal was not considered because of its late arrival.   8._____
   A. This is an example of acceptable writing.
   B. The word "its" should be changed to "it's."
   C. The word "its" should be changed to "the."
   D. The words "late arrival" should be changed to "arrival late."

9. The letter must be read carefuly to determine under which subject it should be filed.   9._____
   A. This is an example of acceptable writing.
   B. The word "under" should be changed to "at."
   C. The word "determine" should be spelled "determin."
   D. The word "carefuly" should be spelled "carefully."

10. He showed potential as an office manager, but he lacked skill in delegating work.   10._____
    A. This is an example of acceptable writing.
    B. The word "delegating" should be spelled "delagating."
    C. The word "potential" should be spelled "potencial."
    D. The words "he lacked" should be changed to "was lacking."

KEY (CORRECT ANSWERS)

1.	D	6.	B
2.	B	7.	A
3.	C	8.	A
4.	D	9.	D
5.	A	10.	A

TEST 2

DIRECTIONS: Each question consists of a sentence which may or may not be an example of good English usage. Examine each sentence, considering grammar, punctuation, spelling, capitalization, and awkwardness. Then choose the correct statement about it from the four choices below it. If the English usage in the sentence given is better than any of the changes suggested in choices B, C, or D, pick choice A. (Do not pick a choice that will change the meaning of the sentence.) *PRINT THE LETTER OF THE CORRECT ANSWER IN THE SPACE AT THE RIGHT.*

1. The supervisor wants that all staff members report to the office at 9:00 A.M.   1.____
   A. This is an example of acceptable writing.
   B. The word "that" should be removed and the word "to" should be inserted after the word "members."
   C. There should be a comma after the word "wants" and a comma after the word "office."
   D. The word "wants" should be changed to "want" and the word "shall" should be inserted after the word "members."

2. Every morning the clerk opens the office mail and distributes it.   2.____
   A. This is an example of acceptable writing.
   B. The word "opens" should be changed to "open."
   C. The word "mail" should be changed to "letters."
   D. The word "it" should be changed to "them."

3. The secretary typed more fast on a desktop computer than on a laptop computer.   3.____
   A. This is an example of acceptable writing.
   B. The words "more fast" should be changed to "faster."
   C. There should be a comma after the words "desktop computer."
   D. The word "than" should be changed to "then."

4. The new stenographer needed a desk a computer, a chair and a blotter.   4.____
   A. This is an example of acceptable writing.
   B. The word "blotter" should be spelled "blodder."
   C. The word "stenographer" should begin with a capital letter.
   D. There should be a comma after the word "desk."

5. The recruiting officer said, "There are many different goverment jobs available."   5.____
   A. This is an example of acceptable writing.
   B. The word "There" should not be capitalized.
   C. The word "government" should be spelled "government."
   D. The comma after the word "said" should be removed.

6. He can recommend a mechanic whose work is reliable.   6.____
   A. This is an example of acceptable writing.
   B. The word "reliable" should be spelled "relyable."
   C. The word "whose" should be spelled "who's."
   D. The word "mechanic should be spelled "mecanic."

7. She typed quickly; like someone who had not a moment to lose. 7._____
   A. This is an example of acceptable writing.
   B. The word "not" should be removed.
   C. The semicolon should be changed to a comma.
   D. The word "quickly" should be placed before instead of after the word "typed."

8. She insisted that she had to much work to do. 8._____
   A. This is an example of acceptable writing.
   B. The word "insisted" should be spelled "incisted."
   C. The word "to" used in front of "much" should be spelled "too."
   D. The word "do" should be changed to "be done."

9. He excepted praise from his supervisor for a job well done. 9._____
   A. This is an example of acceptable writing.
   B. The word "excepted" should be spelled "accepted."
   C. The order of the words "well done" should be changed to "done well."
   D. There should be a comma after the word "supervisor."

10. What appears to be intentional errors in grammar occur several times in the passage. 10._____
    A. This is an example of acceptable writing.
    B. The word "occur" should be spelled "occurr."
    C. The word "appears" should be changed to "appear."
    D. The phrase "several times" should be changed to "from time to time."

KEY (CORRECT ANSWERS)

1.	B	6.	A
2.	A	7.	C
3.	B	8.	C
4.	D	9.	B
5.	C	10.	C

TEST 3

DIRECTIONS: Each question consists of a sentence which may or may not be an example of good English usage. Examine each sentence, considering grammar, punctuation, spelling, capitalization, and awkwardness. Then choose the correct statement about it from the four choices below it. If the English usage in the sentence given is better than any of the changes suggested in choices B, C, or D, pick choice A. (Do not pick a choice that will change the meaning of the sentence.) *PRINT THE LETTER OF THE CORRECT ANSWER IN THE SPACE AT THE RIGHT.*

1. The clerk could have completed the assignment on time if he knows where these materials were located.
    A. This is an example of acceptable writing.
    B. The word "knows" should be replaced by "had known."
    C. The word "were" should be replaced by "had been."
    D. The words "where these materials were located" should be replaced by "the location of these materials."

2. All employees should be given safety training. Not just those who accidents.
    A. This is an example of acceptable writing.
    B. The period after the word "training" should be changed to a colon.
    C. The period after the word "training" should be changed to a semicolon, and the first letter of the word "Not" should be changed to a small "n."
    D. The period after the word "training" should be changed to a comma, and the first letter of the word "Not" should be changed to a small "n."

3. This proposal is designed to promote employee awareness of the suggestion program, to encourage employee participation in the program, and to increase the number of suggestions submitted.
    A. This is an example of acceptable writing.
    B. The word "proposal" should be spelled "proposal."
    C. The words "to increase the number of suggestions submitted" should be changed to "an increase in the number of suggestions is expected."
    D. The word "promote" should be changed to "enhance" and the word "increase" should be changed to "add to."

4. The introduction of inovative managerial techniques should be preceded by careful analysis of the specific circumstances and conditions in each department.
    A. This is an example of acceptable writing.
    B. The word "technique" should be spelled "techneques."
    C. The word "inovative" should be spelled "innovative."
    D. A comma should be placed after the word "circumstances" and after the word "conditions."

175

5. This occurrence indicates that such criticism embarrasses him.
   A. This is an example of acceptable writing.
   B. The word "occurrence" should be spelled "occurence."
   C. The word "criticism" should be spelled "critisism.
   D. The word "embarrasses" should be spelled "embarases.

5.____

KEY (CORRECT ANSWERS)

1. B
2. D
3. A
4. C
5. A

WRITTEN ENGLISH EXPRESSION
EXAMINATION SECTION
TEST 1

DIRECTIONS: In each of the sentences below, four portions are underlined and lettered. Read each sentence and decide whether any of the UNDERLINED parts contains an error in spelling, punctuation, or capitalization, or employs grammatical usage which would be inappropriate for carefully written English. If so, note the letter printed under the unacceptable form and indicate this choice in the space at the right. If all four of the underlined portions are acceptable as they stand, select the answer E. (No sentence contains more than ONE unacceptable form.)

1. The revised <u>procedure</u> was <u>quite</u> different <u>than</u> the one which <u>was</u> employed up to that time. <u>No error</u>
          A   B   C   D   E   1.____

2. <u>Blinded</u> by the storm that <u>surrounded</u> him, his plane <u>kept going</u> in <u>circles</u>. <u>No error</u>
    A   B   C   D   E   2.____

3. They <u>should</u> give the book to <u>whoever</u> <u>they</u> think deserves <u>it</u>. <u>No error</u>
          A   B   C   D E   3.____

4. The <u>government</u> will not consent to your <u>firm</u> <u>sending</u> that package as <u>second class</u> matter. <u>No error</u>
        A   B   C   D   E   4.____

5. She <u>would have</u> avoided all the trouble <u>that</u> followed if she <u>would have</u> waited ten minutes <u>longer</u>. <u>No error</u>
          A   B   C   D   E   5.____

6. <u>His</u> poetry, <u>when</u> it was carefully examined, showed <u>characteristics</u> not unlike <u>Wordsworth</u>. <u>No error</u>
    A   B   C   D   E   6.____

7. <u>In my opinion</u>, based upon long years of research, <u>I think</u> the plan offered by my opponent is <u>unsound</u>, because it is not <u>founded</u> on true facts. <u>No error</u>
         A   B   C   D   E   7.____

8. The soldiers of <u>Washington's</u> army at Valley Forge <u>were</u> men ragged in
                     A   B
   <u>appearance</u> but <u>who were</u> noble in character. <u>No error</u>
      C   D   E

9. Rabbits <u>have a distrust</u> of man <u>due to</u> the fact <u>that</u> they are <u>so often</u> shot.
              A   B   C   D
   <u>No error</u>
    E

10. <u>This</u> is the man <u>who</u> I believe <u>is</u> best <u>qualified</u> for the position. <u>No error</u>
     A   B   C   D   E

11. Her voice was <u>not only</u> <u>good</u>, but <u>she</u> also very clearly <u>enunciated</u>.
                      A   B   C   D
    <u>No error</u>
     E

12. <u>Today he</u> is wearing a <u>different</u> suit <u>than</u> the <u>one</u> he wore yesterday. <u>No error</u>
        A   B   C   D   E

13. Our work <u>is</u> to improve the club; if anybody <u>must</u> resign, let it <u>not</u> be you or <u>I</u>.
               A   B   C   D
    <u>No error</u>
     E

14. There was so much talking <u>in back of</u> me <u>as</u> I <u>could</u> not <u>enjoy</u> the music.
                                       A   B   C   D
    <u>No error</u>
     E

15. <u>Being that</u> he is that <u>kind of</u> <u>boy</u>, he cannot be blamed <u>for</u> the mistake.
       A   B   C   D
    <u>No error</u>
     E

16. <u>The king, having read</u> the speech, <u>he</u> and the <u>queen</u> <u>departed</u>. <u>No error</u>
                   A   B   C   D   E

17. I <u>am</u> <u>so tired</u> I <u>can't</u> <u>scarcely</u> stand. <u>No error</u>
       A   B   C   D   E

18. We are <u>mailing bills</u> to our customers <u>in Canada</u>, and, <u>being</u> eager to
                    A   B   C
    clear our books before the new season opens, it is <u>to be hoped</u> they will
                                                                               D
    send their remittances promptly. <u>No error</u>
                                          E

19. I reluctantly acquiesced to the proposal. No error
    A   B   C   D   E

20. It had lain out in the rain all night. No error
    A   B   C   D   E

21. If he would have gone there, he would have seen a marvelous sight.
                 A   B   C   D
    No error
    E

22. The climate of Asia Minor is somewhat like Utah. No error
                 A   B   C   D   E

23. If everybody did unto others as they would wish others to do unto them, this
          A   B   C   D
    world would be a paradise. No error
                                E

24. This was the jockey whom I saw was most likely to win the race. No error
        A   B   C   D   E

25. The only food the general demanded was potatoes. No error
        A   B   C   D   E

KEY (CORRECT ANSWERS)

1. C   11. C
2. A   12. C
3. B   13. D
4. B   14. B
5. C   15. A

6. D   16. A
7. B   17. C
8. D   18. C
9. B   19. E
10. E   20. E

21. A
22. D
23. D
24. B
25. E

TEST 2

DIRECTIONS: In each of the sentences below, four portions are underlined and lettered. Read each sentence and decide whether any of the UNDERLINED parts contains an error in spelling, punctuation, or capitalization, or employs grammatical usage which would be inappropriate for carefully written English. If so, note the letter printed under the unacceptable form and indicate this choice in the space at the right. If all four of the underlined portions are acceptable as they stand, select the answer E. (No sentence contains more than ONE unacceptable form.)

1. A party <u>like</u> <u>that</u> <u>only</u> <u>comes</u> once a year. <u>No error</u>
         A   B   C   D   E
1.____

2. <u>Our's</u> <u>is</u> <u>a swift moving</u> age. <u>No error</u>
  A   B C   D   E
2.____

3. The <u>healthy</u> climate soon <u>restored</u> him <u>to</u> his <u>accustomed</u> vigor. <u>No error</u>
      A   B   C   D   E
3.____

4. <u>They</u> needed six typists and hoped that <u>only</u> that <u>many</u> <u>would</u> apply for the position. <u>No error</u>
  A   B   C   D
               E
4.____

5. He <u>interviewed</u> people <u>whom</u> he thought had <u>something</u> <u>to impart</u>. <u>No error</u>
     A   B   C   D   E
5.____

6. <u>Neither</u> of his three sisters <u>is</u> older <u>than</u> <u>he</u>. <u>No error</u>
    A   B   C D   E
6.____

7. <u>Since</u> he is <u>that</u> <u>kind</u> of <u>a</u> boy, he cannot be expected to cooperate with us. <u>No error</u>
   A   B   C   D
   E
7.____

8. <u>When passing</u> <u>through</u> the tunnel, the air pressure <u>affected</u> <u>our</u> years. <u>No error</u>
      A   B   C   D   E
8,____

9. <u>The story having</u> a sad ending, <u>it</u> never <u>achieved</u> popularity <u>among</u> the students. <u>No error</u>
    A   B   C   D
           E
9.____

10. <u>Since</u> we are both hungry, <u>shall</u> we go <u>somewhere</u> for lunch? <u>No error</u>
    A   B   C   D E
10.____

11. Will you please bring this book down to the library and give it to my friend,   11._____
    A   B   C   D
    who is waiting for it? No error
                            E

12. You may have the book; I am finished with it. No error   12._____
        A   B   C   D   E

13. I don't know if I should mention it to her or not. No error   13._____
      A   B   C   D   E

14. Philosophy is not a subject which has to do with philosophers and   14._____
                    A   B   C
    mathematics only. No error
                D   E

15. The thoughts of the scholar in his library are little different than the old woman   15._____
                                 A   B
    who first said, "It's no use crying over spilt milk." No error
                 C   D   E

16. A complete system of philosophical ideas are implied in many simple   16._____
                A   B   C
    utterances. No error
        D   E

17. Even if one has never put them into words, his ideas compose a kind of a   17._____
          A   B   C   D
    philosophy. No error
                  E

18. Perhaps it is well enough that most people do not attempt this formulation.   18._____
              A   B   C   D
    No error
      E

19. Leading their ordered lives, this confused body of ideas and feelings is   19._____
         A   B   C   D
    sufficient. No error
                  E

20. Why should we insist upon them formulating it? No error   20._____
         A   B   C   D   E

21. Since it includes something of the wisdom of the ages, it is adequate for the   21._____
      A   B   C
    purposes of ordinary life. No error
        D   E

22. Therefore, I have sought to make a pattern of mine, and so there were, early
            A   B   C
    moments of my trying to find out what were the elements with which I had to
              D
    deal. No error
          E

23. I wanted to get what knowledge I could about the general structure of the
      A   B   C   D
    universe. No error
              E

24. I wanted to know if life per se had any meaning or whether I must strive to give
                  A B   C   D
    it one. No error
            E

25. So, in a desultory way, I began to read. No error
    A   B   C   D   E

KEY (CORRECT ANSWERS)

1.	C		11.	B
2.	A		12.	C
3.	A		13.	B
4.	C		14.	D
5.	B		15.	B
6.	A		16.	B
7.	D		17.	A
8.	A		18.	C
9.	A		19.	A
10.	E		20.	D

21. E
22. C
23. C
24. B
25. E